Published on the Fund Established
in Memory of Ganson Goodyear Depew

THE INNS OF COURT AND EARLY ENGLISH DRAMA

By A. Wigfall Green
With a Preface by Roscoe Pound
Dean of the Harvard Law School

New Haven, Yale University Press
London, Humphrey Milford, Oxford University Press
1931

Printed in the United States of America

"Lawyers, I suppose, were children once."

CHARLES LAMB

The Old Benchers of the Inner Temple.

Preface

HERE is a book which touches many interests stirring in the life of today. This is a time of insistence upon interrelations. Points of contact are emphasized where a generation ago we neglected the periphery of institutions and looked exclusively at the core of what in consequence seemed unrelated, self-sufficient activities. As coöperation takes a larger place in the general consciousness, as compared with competition, we look more at the relational aspects of life. The Middle Ages, the era of relational organization of society, become significant, not merely as showing us institutions in embryo, as we used to think, but as showing us a society in many ways analogous to what seems to be developing in a new economic and social order.

There was little to interest Americans of the last century in the immemorial self-governing societies of English lawyers. Mr. Weasel, who could debate with a puzzled proctor, as an abstract question, the proper situs for administration while attending his aunt's funeral, and could see in the parable of the unjust steward, when read in church, a suggestive exercise in the respective jurisdictions of law and chancery, was a type more intelligible to the unorganized bar of individual money-getters in the last century than the enlightened patrons of letters in the Inns of Court of Renaissance and Reformation England, or than the philosopher who rose to the highest place on the English bench while taking all knowledge for his province. It is true lawyers were never wholly craftsmen, even in the nadir of professional feeling in nineteenth-century America. There is an intimate relation between law and politics throughout the English-speaking world, and this relation was particularly strong with us in the last century. Later there came to be a growing intimacy between law and business. But it remains true that narrowed interests of individuals were as characteristic of the latter part of the last century as broad interests of groups of men working in coöperation are of today. Thus a book which tells a bit of legal history and a bit of literary history, not exclusively as either, but as parts of one story, is in the spirit of the time.

But I must speak primarily for the lawyer. The conception of a body of men united in the pursuit of a common calling as a learned art, and pursuing it in the spirit of a public service rather than as an individual means of livelihood, ran counter to all the instincts of the pioneer in the new world and of the democracy of our formative period. The idea of a common life lived by those coöperating in such a calling, the idea expressed in religious houses and craft guilds, was an anachronism in an age which thought of a maximum of competitive, acquisitive self-assertion as the highest good. It is significant that there is a strong revival of interest in the Middle Ages and in medieval institutions, and that ideas of coöperation and relation and organization are stirring after centuries of abeyance.

In the formative era of American institutions we went far toward deprofessionalizing the professions. The present century, on the other hand, has seen a reprofessionalizing of medicine, and the beginnings of a reprofessionalizing of law in the United States are manifest everywhere. Hence whatever has to do with the Inns of Court has an interest for lawyers, not merely as a part of the history of our law, but as helping toward a starting point for thought, as we feel the need of organization and self-discipline and collective responsibility; as we feel the need of developing the collective professional spirit in contrast to the individual and competitive spirit.

Moreover, the interest of the lawyer in these medieval self-governing societies of lawyers should not stop with the

Middle Ages. There is much to teach us in the continuity of their history from the relationally organized society of pre-Reformation England through the centuries of individualism into the rising relational social organization of today. The activities of these societies at the end of the sixteenth century and beginning of the seventeenth century, on the eve of colonization, require us to think why, when we received other English legal institutions so completely, we rejected these.

It is noteworthy that the classical era of the common law was a classical literary era. It was an age of discovery, adventure, and economic and political development. What lawyers were doing in such times outside of their moots and readings and pleadings, may suggest something in a like time of discovery and adventure and transition, in which the bar is moving toward a self-governing responsible organization, conscious of collective duties and possibilities. Indeed, the rise of a new spirit among American lawyers is shown by such things as the recent pageant of Magna Charta under the auspices of the American Bar Association. In that frame of mind we may read profitably of a time when it was not a matter of individual lawyers devoted to letters, but of whole bodies of lawyers devoted collectively as well as individually to the raising of human powers to their highest possible unfolding in all the things of the spirit.

No one would think seriously of attempting to restore or to imitate exactly these societies of lawyers as they were in their great days, or to attempt to do exactly what they did in the past. Yet we may learn from them something of what an organized profession, a body of men carrying on a great calling in the grand style, may do for civilization at large as well as for their immediate task.

ROSCOE POUND.

Washington, D. C.
June 1, 1931.

Contents

PREFACE by Roscoe Pound — vii

LIST OF ILLUSTRATIONS — xiii

CHAPTER I. The Inns of Court and English Literature — 1

CHAPTER II. Rise of the Inns of Court and Their Internal Organization — 22

CHAPTER III. Professional Revels — 40
- (a) The Reader's Feast — 40
- (b) The Sergeants' Feast — 48

CHAPTER IV. Political Revels — 53

CHAPTER V. Ecclesiastical Revels — 55
- (a) The Feasts of All Saints and the Purification — 55
- (b) Christmas Celebration — 56

CHAPTER VI. The Masque — 97
- (a) The Masque of 1526 — 97
- (b) Masques of 1565–66 and 1592 — 98
- (c) *The Masque of Proteus* — 98
- (d) *The Masque of the Nine Passions* — 102
- (e) *The Masque of the Middle Temple and Lincoln's Inn* — 102
- (f) *The Masque of the Inner-Temple and Gray's Inn* — 105
- (g) *The Masque of Flowers* — 109
- (h) *The Inner Temple Masque*, or *Ulysses and Circe* — 112
- (i) *The Masque of Mountebanks* — 117
- (j) *The Inner Temple Masque*, or *The Masque of Heroes* — 121
- (k) *The Triumph of Peace* — 123
- (l) *The Triumphs of the Prince d'Amour* — 132
- (m) Gray's Inn Masque of February 2, 1683 — 135
- (n) Miscellaneous Masques — 136

CHAPTER VII. Miscellaneous Entertainment — 137
- (a) Creation of Charles as Prince of Wales — 137
- (b) The Dance of the Nations — 138

CHAPTER VIII. The Drama 142
(a) *Gorboduc* 142
(b) *Jocasta* 145
(c) *The Supposes* 146
(d) *Tancred and Gismund* 147
(e) *The Misfortunes of Arthur* 150
(f) Miscellaneous Plays 153
APPENDICES
Appendix A 161
Appendix B 163
Appendix C 167
Appendix D 168
Appendix E 171
BIBLIOGRAPHY 183
INDEX 189

Illustrations

Autographs of Illustrious Personages Entertained at Lincoln's Inn Hall on February 29, 1671 — 42

(From *The Student's Guide through Lincoln's Inn*, by Thomas Lane.)

Entertainment of Charles II at One of the Inns — 64

(From *Christmas*, by W. F. Dawson.)

Bringing in the Boar's Head — 64

(From *Christmas*, by W. F. Dawson.)

Sir Francis Bacon — 112

(From *Origines Juridiciales*, by William Dugdale.)

The Temple and Temple Stairs — 136

(From *Good Company in Old Westminster and the Temple*, by Constance Hill, published by John Lane, The Bodley Head Limited, London.)

Ticket of Admission to a Masque at Gray's Inn Hall — 136

(From *The Progresses and Public Processions of Queen Elizabeth &c.*, by John Nichols.)

Sir Christopher Hatton — 148

(From *Origines Juridiciales*, by William Dugdale.)

CHAPTER I

The Inns of Court and English Literature

A RATHER advanced sense of humor permits the Englishman to smile, and even to jeer, at national institutions which he holds dear to his heart. The English legal system has been the subject of derision for centuries, but no good Englishman would for a moment consider seriously either its destruction or its material alteration. Fortunately, this form of entertainment is not confined to lay folk; the lawyers themselves enjoy it quite as much as others. Much of the diversion of the members of the Inns of Court, and particularly of the students, during the sixteenth and seventeenth centuries, consisted in satirizing legal forms, procedure, and personages. During the holiday season, the young gentlemen were given *carte blanche*. Often the four Inns, with their subsidiary Inns of Chancery, joined together for the purpose of ridiculing their superiors. This practice, which is probably a survival of an ancient Greek custom of permitting servants on one day of each year to exchange places with their masters, may be found in some of the older law schools of America. The various legal fraternities unite to ridicule the administration of the law school, methods of teaching the law, and anomalies in the practice of the law. The faculty is dominated by the students, who mock their imperfections and idiosyncrasies; legal doctrines, like that of the "last clear chance" or that of "avulsion and accretion," are expounded humorously. In general, however, the American legal system—notwithstanding some few alliterative catch phrases about lawyers—is taken rather seriously, particularly by those who are engaged in the practice of the law. It is commonly thought that American jurisprudence is indigenous, the product of some few statutes which were introduced by inspired patriots, or the reflection of some few heroic characters like John Marshall or Abraham Lincoln, both of whom were largely self-taught in the law. It is to the Inns of Court however, that America, as well as England, is indebted: Thomas Littleton, John Fortescue, Edward Coke, Francis Bacon, and William Blackstone, whose works are used for reference in American law schools today, were all students at the Inns of Court, and their interpretation and expansion of English laws have inevitably affected the American judicial system. The law of the United States is based upon both statute and precedent: American laws, in many cases, embody reënactments of English statutes; and American precedent, particularly in Massachusetts, Virginia, and Maryland, and the others of the thirteen original colonies, often rests upon decisions of English jurists and pleas of English lawyers. The governmental relationship between England and the United States is quite as great as the legal. Many of the men who shaped the form of government for the new democracy were products of the Inns of Court: five of the signers of the Declaration of Independence, five of the members of the Continental Congress which adopted the Articles of Confederation, and six of the signatories of the Constitution of the United States were Middle Templars.

A great indebtedness of both England and America to the Inns of Court—one which has not yet been fully realized even by England—lies in literature, especially in dramatic literature. During the sixteenth and seventeenth centuries particularly, the curriculum at the Inns of Court, or perhaps the lack of it, stimulated writing. Many of the young lawyers thought, with Disraeli, that the law depresses but that literature exalts. The placidity of the Inns rendered them an ideal rendezvous for poets, dramatists, and novelists, and many of the juvenilia, as well as many of the masterpieces, of authors were conceived within the four houses. Residents

Temple Masque; Francis Beaumont, author of the masque presented by the Inner Temple and Gray's Inn; William Wycherley, Arthur Henry Hallam, Thomas Hughes, and James Boswell. Charles Lamb said, "I was born, and passed the first seven years of my life, in the Temple."[4]

At the Middle Temple resided John Evelyn, William Congreve, Oliver Goldsmith, who is buried in the graveyard there, Thomas de Quincey, and William Cowper. The two greatest nineteenth-century novelists lived for some time at the Inns. One of them, Thackeray, obtained much of his material for *Pendennis* at the Middle Temple: chapter xxix, "The Knights of the Temple," presents a rather good picture of the Inns:

A well-ordained workhouse or prison is much better provided with the appliances of health, comfort, and cleanliness, than a Foundation School, a venerable College, or a learned Inn. In the latter place of residence men are contented to sleep in dingy closets, and to pay for sitting-room and the cupboard, which is their dormitory, the price of a good villa and garden in the suburbs, or of a roomy house in the neglected square of the town. . . . Nevertheless those venerable Inns which have the Lamb and Flag and the Winged Horse for their signs, have attractions for the persons who inhabit them, and a share of rough comfort and freedom, which men always remember with pleasure. I don't know whether the student of Law permits himself the refreshment of enthusiasm, or indulges in poetical reminiscences as he passes by historical chambers, and says, "Yonder Eldon lived—upon this side Coke mused upon Lyttleton—here Chitty toiled—here Barnwell and Alderson joined in their famous labors—here Byles composed his great work upon Bills, and Smith compiled his Immortal Leading Cases—here Gustavus still toils, with Solomon to aid him"; but the man of letters can't but love the place which has been inhabited by so many of his brethren, or peopled by their creations as real to us at this day as the authors whose children they were—and Sir Roger de Coverly walking in the Temple Garden, and discoursing with Mr. Spectator about the

[4] "The Older Benchers of the Inner Temple."

beauties in hoops and patches who are sauntering over the grass, is just as lively a figure to me as old Samuel Johnson rolling through the fog with the Scotch gentleman at his heels on their way to Dr. Goldsmith's chambers in Brick Court; or Henry Fielding, with inked ruffles, and a wet towel round his head, dashing off articles at midnight for the Covent Garden Journal, while the printer's boy is asleep in the passage.

Shakespeare's *Twelfth Night* was presented in the Middle Temple Hall in 1602.

Spenser says of the Temple:

> There when they came, whereas those bricky towres,
> The which on Themmes brode aged backe doe ryde,
> Where now the studious lawyers have their bowers,
> There whylome wont the Templar Knights to byde,
> Till they decayd through pride:[5]

Lincoln's Inn produced Sir Thomas More. Ben Jonson, who, it is said, assisted his stepfather in the building of a wall at Lincoln's Inn, dedicated *Every Man Out of His Humor* to "the noblest nurseries of humanity and liberty, the INNS OF COURT." Samuel Butler, who according to tradition attended one of the Inns, describes the barristers at Lincoln's Inn as those who

> Retain all sorts of witnesses
> That ply i' th' Temples under trees,
> Or walk the Round[6] with Knights o' th' Posts
> About their cross-legged knights their hosts,
> Or wait for customers between
> The pillar-rows in Lincoln's Inn.[7]

In *Clarissa Harlowe*,[8] Lovelace visits Lincoln's Inn chapel in the hope of finding there the "fair creature." Jeremy Bentham began taking his dinners at Lincoln's Inn during 1763. Thomas B. Macaulay, Edward Bulwer-Lytton,

[5] "Prothalamion," pp. 130–136.
[6] Ambulatory.
[7] "Hudibras," III, Canto 3.
[8] By Samuel Richardson.

Charles Kingsley, and William Wilkie Collins were also residents at Lincoln's.

Among the famous persons who had chambers at Gray's Inn are George Gascoigne, author of *Jocasta* and *The Supposes,* who earlier resided at the Middle Temple. Sir Philip Sidney became a member of this fashionable Inn when he was twelve years old. Perhaps the most famous graduate of Gray's was Sir Francis Bacon who, besides the speeches of the six councilors of the *Gesta Graiorum,* wrote speeches for various devices and mummings; he was the "chief contriver" of the masque by Francis Beaumont presented at the marriage of Princess Elizabeth, and the "chief encourager" of the *Masque of Flowers.*[9] As his most important biographer says, "On high-days and holidays he assisted with great glee in all the festivities of the Inn; and at the request of the Benchers he laid out walks in the garden, and planted trees."[10] In his essay "Of Masques and Triumphs," Bacon says, however: "These things are but toys . . . but yet, since princes will have such things, it is better that they should be graced with elegancy than daubed with cost." When his honor had been impugned by the world, Bacon found solace once more at Gray's Inn. George Chapman, who resided there, was the author of the masque presented by the Middle Temple and Lincoln's Inn at the marriage of Princess Elizabeth. John Cleveland, Thomas Rymer, and William Camden were likewise products of this Inn. Samuel Johnson, who wrote *Rasselas* at Staple Inn, had chambers at Gray's in 1759. Dryden's *Sir Martin Mar-all,* like numerous other plays and novels, contains references to this Inn. Charles Dickens, the other of the great nineteenth-century novelists,[11] was apprenticed to Mr. Blackmore, a solicitor of Gray's Inn.

[9] Fleay, *Chronicle of the English Drama,* I, 1592 to 1614; Fletcher, Introduction, pp. 16–17.

[10] Campbell, *The Life of Lord Bacon,* p. 14.

[11] See p. 5.

His experiences there are recorded in practically all his works, but especially in his autobiographical novel, *David Copperfield*; in chapter xxxi of *The Posthumous Papers of the Pickwick Club*, entitled "Which Is All about the Law, and Sundry Great Authorities Learned Therein"; and in chapter xv of *Barnaby Rudge*, as follows:

> There are, still, worse places than the Temple, on a sultry day, for basking in the sun, or resting idly in the shade. There is yet a drowsiness in its courts, and a dreamy dulness in its trees and gardens; those who pace its lanes and squares may yet hear the echoes of their footsteps on the sounding stones, and read upon its gates, in passing from the tumult of the Strand or Fleet Street, "Who enters here leaves noise behind." There is still the plash of falling water in fair Fountain Court, and there are yet nooks and corners where dun-haunted students may look down from their dusty garrets, on a vagrant ray of sunlight patching the shade of the tall houses, and seldom troubled to reflect a passing stranger's form. There is yet, in the Temple, something of a clerkly monkish atmosphere, which public offices of law have not disturbed, and even legal firms have failed to scare away. In summer time, its pumps suggest to thirsty idlers, springs cooler, and more sparkling, and deeper than other wells; and as they trace the spillings of full pitchers on the heated ground, they snuff the freshness, and, sighing, cast sad looks towards the Thames, and think of baths and boats, and saunter on, despondent.

Shakespeare's *Comedy of Errors* was presented in Gray's Inn Hall in 1594.

The inevitable outcome, in a literary atmosphere, of a penchant for jesting at custom was the creation of a literature peculiar to the Inns of Court. The Inns were, in effect, the legal guild of England, superior of course to the merchant and trade guilds, because the gentlemen of the Inns were of the social and intellectual aristocracy. Nevertheless, their tradition was much the same as that of the crafts: they had chaplains and temples in which to worship. Spenser says in his "Faerie Queene," II, 7:

> The room was large and wide,
> As it some Guild or solemn Temple were.

Like the guildsmen, who transacted business in the crypt supported by columns beneath the hall, the gentlemen of the Inns consulted with their clients in the ambulatory beneath the temple hall. Guilds were originally associations for defense and for the propagation of Christianity, including the dispensing of charity. Their chaplains, in order to instruct better, taught the members to repeat portions of Biblical stories; on holidays, and particularly on Corpus Christi Day, legends from the Bible were performed on mobile stages; sometimes many guilds united and performed all the more important legends, from the creation to the day of judgment; thus was gradually originated the English miracle and mystery play. This fondness for the drama was part of the heritage of the Inns of Court from the merchant and trade guilds. A more important dramatic inheritance was, perhaps, received from the Knights Templars, whose monastic buildings the lawyers and law students occupied after the disestablishment of monasteries by Henry VIII. Many of the customs of the Templars were adopted by the lawyers, who came likewise to be called Templars. This dramatic tradition, which rests largely upon religious ritual, is entirely distinct from that of the guildsmen. But even more remotely, the dramatic tradition of the Inns of Court had its origin in the pagan agricultural feast, much of the ceremonial of which has been transmitted through the Christmas celebration of the Inns of Court. From the ritual of that feast rose the pageant, which was later blended with the ceremonial of the Christian pageant. Both the law and religion have ever fostered the fine arts, and particularly the drama; but the law has not been so much circumscribed by its nature as has the church, so that it has, in one sense, done more to stimulate the drama. When the Knights Templars were officers of the church, their entertainment, although lavish, was usually religious. However, with the rise of the Inns of Court, entertainment, although colored by religious tradition, became distinctive as it became tinctured with ceremonial peculiar to the law profession. So, the legal pageant grew to be coördinate with the religious pageant.

The most scenic of the revels were held on holy days, of which the more important ones observed were the feast of All Saints or All Hallows (All-hallown), the feast of the Purification or Candlemas or Ground-hog day, and Ascension day. Originally even the birthdays of the most insignificant saints were kept; thus much of the year was devoted to feasting and revelry. It was therefore decreed at Lincoln's Inn, in 9 Henry VI (1431), that "there ſhould be four Revells that year, and no more; one at the feaſt of All-hallown, another at the feaſt of St. Erkenwald; the third at the feaſt of the Purification of our Lady; and the 4th on Midſummer day."[12]

The royalty and nobility were guests at these revels just as they were at the readers' and sergeants' feasts. In 1670, Charles II, "the Prince of Orange, with other Dukes and Duchesses, were incog. at the Revels at Lincoln's Inn, and its thought the Queen and some of the Duchesses will be there next Saturday."[13]

A small portion of these holy days was devoted to church attendance and to prayer, with special invocation to the Lord upon the Inns of Court.[14] The gentlemen of the societies were enjoined to attend "Maſs, Matens, Evenſongs, &c. . . . and keep xviii Offering days in the year, according to the antient laudable Cuſtome of this Houſe."[15] Sermons were usually delivered by prominent ministers engaged by the houses at an annual stipend;[16] moreover, distinguished ministers and bishops having no connection with the Inns

[12] Dugdale, p. 246.
[13] Black Book, III, 450.
[14] Bellot, pp. 36–38.
[15] Dugdale, p. 148.
[16] Inderwick, I, 434.

were invited to preach on special occasions.[17] During the late seventeenth century, these special sermons seem to have been largely on atheism and revelation.[18] Usually, however, most of the "grand days" were devoted to eating, singing, and dancing.[19]

The records of the Inner Temple show that, as early as 1505, a master of the revels (*magister jocorum*) was chosen at the Inner Temple. It is probable that the master of the revels existed at the Inns before he was known at Oxford or Cambridge, although this fact may not be established definitively. At Trinity College, Cambridge, which was not founded until 1546, we find among the statutes a chapter entitled "De Praefecto Ludorum qui Imperator dicitur." This officer at Trinity produced comedies and tragedies, usually from the Latin, much as they were produced at the Inns of Court. The election of the master of the revels is probably the survival of an English community custom of ancient origin. Many noblemen, during the sixteenth and seventeenth centuries appointed, within their own houses, similar officers. Queen Elizabeth's master of the revels was an officer of dignity; his office was on a parity with that of the lieutenant of the Tower.[20] The master of the revels[21] at

[17] The Bishop of Rochester was tendered an elaborate dinner by the Templars when he preached at the reopening of the Temple church (Inderwick, III, 199).

[18] Melmoth (Appendix) lists the following Boyle lecturers: 1692, Dr. Richard Bentley, "A Confutation of Atheism." 1693, 1694, Bishop Kidder, "A Demonstration of the Messias." This forms part of his larger work afterward published under that title. 1695, 1696, Bishop Williams, "On Divine Revelation." 8vo, 1708. 1698, Dr. J. Harris, "A Refutation of Atheistical Objections against the Being and Attributes of God." 4to, 1698.

[19] Sometimes the musicians received an annual salary; at other times they were specially employed (Fletcher, II, 14). In February, 1589–90, the musicians played for two nights and one day (Inderwick, I, 363). (See also Herbert, p. 314, and Dugdale, p. 246.)

[20] Stopes, *Seventeenth Century Revels*, p. 5; Bodleian MS clxviii, p. 120.

[21] Sometimes called the lord of misrule, although, in some cases, this officer is distinct from the master of the revels.

each of the Inns was likewise an officer of considerable importance, who had almost entire control of entertainment on festive occasions. He was often assisted by the steward who, by virtue of his office, was entitled to wear a gold chain of the value of one hundred marks. Sometimes, of course, other officers of the revels were elected to take precedence over the master; a king was often elected for service on Christmas and New Year's days, and a king of cockneys on Childermas day.[22]

On these holidays, judges, sergeants, masters of the bench, and barristers attended the celebration, which was led by the master of the revels. A gentleman of the utter bar was customarily designated to sing to the officers, in default of which he was amerced; this song was preceded and followed by highly ritualistic "solemn revels," marked by obeisance and stately parade, and then followed the post revels[23] or informal dancing by the gentlemen of the inner bar.[24] This form of entertainment, which was arranged by the students, was insisted upon by the officers. At Lincoln's Inn, in 7 Jac. I (1610), "the under-barristers were by decimation put out of commons, for example's sake, because the whole bar were offended by not dancing on the Candlemas day preceding, according to the ancient order of this society, when the judges were present."[25]

Into this rather standardized form of entertainment, considerably like that of the readers' and sergeants' feasts, was eventually introduced pageantry and sometimes a play.[26] Buffoonery and burlesque also became popular. In this way

[22] "He and all his Officers ſhould uſe honeſt manner and good Order, without any waſte or deſtruction making, in wine, brawn, Chely, or other Vitails" (Dugdale, pp. 246–247).

[23] In 1568, Lincoln's Inn spent £3 *6s.* *8d.* for "victuals" in entertainment of its ancient ally, the Middle Temple, at post revels (Bellot, p. 313).

[24] Dugdale, p. 161.

[25] Herbert, p. 315.

[26] Numerous items of expenditure for celebration on St. Thomas' Eve and other similar days appear in the records of all the Inns.

the original ritual and revelry gradually took on a dramatic form. The masque and the Latin heroic play, which supplanted to a large extent puerile travesty, were in the ascendant during the early seventeenth century.

As solemn, ritualistic celebration palled with the lawyers, they introduced parody and burlesque of customs and traditions of the law. Such travesty, bringing with it much native comedy, was coarsely salacious, but it helped to form the foundations of a native drama. Although at times the residents of the Inns reveal themselves in these celebrations as little more than imagoes, their dramatic product is usually the thoroughly natural and spontaneous work of young men with a zest for living. The very piquancy of their product shows a fondness for both the incongruous and the beautiful.

Professional revels at the Inns of Court usually consisted in drinking, feasting, and jollification, occasioned by promotion in rank of any one of the members of the Inns. The word "revel" (cf. *reveller*, riot) today means merrymaking or boisterous festivity. During the reign of Elizabeth it meant dancing,[27] or banqueting, or pageantry, masking, and mumming. At professional revels, the part of the host was assumed by a person chosen for the office. Naturally, each member, because he was benefited thereby, anticipated pleasantly the honoring of any other member. Conversely, slight violations of the tradition of the house resulted in amercement of the offending member, the fine being used for the entertainment of the whole house. New members in particular were mulcted: if they were not bedeviled into the commission of some offense, they were penalized for the omission of some duty; inevitably they furnished a "garnish of wine" for their fellows. The accounts of the various Inns seem, at times, to be little more than records of assessments.

[27] "Lincoln's Inn had anciently its dancings or revels allowed at particular seasons" (Herbert, p. 314). See also Welsford, p. 360.

Members newly called to the bar[28] often entertained; and completion of study in a prescribed course frequently terminated in relaxation which might be called a general guzzling. Some of the professional revels were accompanied by great ceremony. Much of the efficacy of the law, as of the church, must be attributed to the majesty and dignity which it has maintained throughout its history. Its very grandeur is what has assured its exalted position. The use of ritual in the law, as in the church, has contributed much to its power. In the professional festivities, ritual is combined abundantly with revelry.

As the law profession became host to royalty and nobility, it altered somewhat its form of entertainment, favoring particularly the masque, which bears genetic relationship to the pageant. Perhaps the first truly native masque was produced by the Inns of Court, and called *The Masque of Amity* because it was devised almost extemporaneously in 1594 by the gentlemen of Gray's Inn to conciliate their native allies, the gentlemen of the Inner Temple. Representing as it does all the famous friendships of history, it reveals not only a good knowledge of history but also unusual dramatic ability. The most spectacular masque ever presented in England is probably *The Triumph of Peace*, devised by James Shirley for the four Inns of Court. The lawyers adopted largely the form of masque which had been gilded at the courts of Italy and France; this form they domesticated and made appropriate to the occasion. They retained not only the most distinguished masque writers in the realm, but also the architect Inigo Jones, whose ingenuity in stagecraft has not been equaled to the present day.

The masque, like the barriers and the installation of the prince, was one of the popular forms of Christmas enter-

[28] Admission usually consisted merely in taking the oath of supremacy at the cupboard; originally students were called to the bar by the reader, but later by order of the parliament, or governing body, of the Inn.

tainment at the Inns of Court.[29] It was probably evolved from ancient mumming, in which the participants, disguised in masks which made them look like animals[30] or birds[31] or exotic human beings, called *en masse* upon their neighbors for the purpose of dancing and dicing. The masque, then, is also an elaborated folk custom,[32] having its origin in the scenic display and the stately magical dance of the primitive agricultural feast.[33]

The masque is a courtly entertainment, with little theme or plot,[34] in which the initial situation must be accepted without challenge. It is usually produced to celebrate an occasion, such as a wedding,[35] a marriage anniversary, or a birthday; sometimes it is of political significance,[36] but very often it is no more than a graceful tribute to the sovereign or to some nobleman. Being, therefore, occasional in its nature, it is usually of only transitory interest. Some of its attributes are lavish display of precious jewels, rich costumes, and ornate settings.[37] The masque is usually produced in a pastoral atmosphere; often the scene is Arcadia or Olympus.

[29] The masque was often presented on those days which formerly had been popular with the mummers: Christmas, the Epiphany, Shrove Tuesday, Candlemas, and May Day (Welsford, p. 9).

[30] Antimasques of baboons will be considered later.

[31] Antimasques of owls were often popular.

[32] Welsford, p. 20.

[33] A modern survival, or revival, of this ritualistic agricultural celebration may be found in the annual apple blossom festival held in Virginia.

[34] The masque usually has no climax or crisis, and no *dénouement* or catastrophe.

[35] The masques presented by the Inns at the marriage of Princess Elizabeth to the Elector Palatine will be discussed later, as will the *Masque of Flowers* in celebration of the wedding of Lady Essex and the Earl of Somerset.

[36] *The Triumph of Peace* was presented as a remonstrance against the publication of William Prynne's *Histriomastix.*

[37] *The Triumph of Peace,* presented before Charles I by the four Inns of Court cost from £21,000 to £24,000, or nearly a million dollars in American money of today.

The characters are frequently mythological. Dancing and instrumental and vocal music are almost indispensable.[38]

The magnificent courts of the late Tudors and the Stuarts naturally fostered this spectacular form of entertainment. As early as 1513, Hall[39] tells us that "the kyng with a xi other were disguised, after the maner of Italie, called a maske, a thyng not seen afore in Englande, thei were apareled in garmentes long and brode, wrought all with gold."[40] The fondness of Elizabeth and of Charles II for ostentation, which was permitted by the general prosperity of the times and the tendency toward extravagance, made them fond of the masque. And also its undramatic but pretentious display rendered it a facile form of compliment to the crown by the young gentlemen of the Inns. A masque could be written on short notice by one of the law students who had a fondness for mythology or Utopianism. Because of the affluence of the Inns and the rapid increase in membership, this costly form of entertainment could be produced without great financial burden to the students individually. The cordial relationship existing between the Inns and the royalty and nobility made this form of pastime appropriate and graceful, without being familiar. So the Inns of Court, housing many gentlemen in the service of the crown, performed their devoir to the sovereign with the masque, gradually relinquishing the older feculent form of entertainment, which had begun to pall. Moreover, the composition and production of masques, like dancing or riding in the tournament, was considered a gentlemanly form of diversion. Dexterity and facility were more important in preparing this gracile recreation than was real dramatic ability. Perhaps

[38] See Welsford, p. 256, and Inderwick, II, xxxviii–xxxix, for excellent descriptions of the masque.

[39] *Chronicle*, p. 256.

[40] The masque came to England from Italy, perhaps by way of France, where it was sometimes presented at carnivals.

nowhere in England could more urbane and complaisant young men be found than at the Inns of Court; certainly the great universities, which were at this time somewhat democratic, offered little competition. With the introduction of the masque, this form of entertainment became very popular at court. At the end of the seventeenth century, when the masque began to cloy, renewed interest was displayed in the drama proper. Although strollers and even actors from the metropolitan companies seem to have been treated with condescension at the Inns,[41] as indicated by their being placed at separate tables, dramatists and masque writers and producers were esteemed by the legal profession, which was complimented by the preparation of ornate scenery by Inigo Jones and by the composition of masques, for presentation by the law students, by William Browne, Thomas Middleton, William Davenant, and Francis Beaumont, some of whom were residents at the Inns. It was particularly appropriate that the Inns of Court, which were training schools for courtiers, should have determined the nature of entertainment for the crown.

In the drama proper, however, the Inns of Court have even more priorities. *Gorboduc*, the first English tragedy, the first play in which blank verse is used, and the first play to employ native legendary material, is the product of the Inns, as are *Jocasta*, perhaps the first adaptation of a Greek play to the English stage; *The Supposes*, the first English prose comedy;[42] *Tancred and Gismund*, the oldest extant

[41] The feeling, which was somewhat general during the sixteenth and seventeenth centuries, that the professional actor was tainted because he followed his art for profit was rather strong at the Inns, where the gentlemen acted for amusement only.

[42] Charles Mills Gayley, in *Representative English Comedies* (New York: The Macmillan Company, 1903), lxxxiv, says: "If it were not for the fact that *The Supposes* (acted 1566) is a translation of Ariosto's play of the same title, I should be inclined to say that it was the first English comedy in every way worthy of the name. It certainly is, for many reasons, entitled to be

play having its source in an Italian *novella*, a source resorted to frequently by the Elizabethan playwright; and *The Misfortunes of Arthur*, the first English play to make use of the Arthurian legend.

It is entirely fitting that English classical drama also should have been born at the Inns of Court. During the sixteenth century the law schools sponsored liberal study of the classics as did no other places of learning in England. At the great universities, at this time, the curricula were highly formalized, and, although they required the study of the classics, existing methods permitted little creative work. The universities were at a disadvantage, moreover, in that they were at a distance from the court, where taste in all the arts was determined. As the gentlemen of the Inns of Court were usually of families of higher rank than were the students at the universities, they were naturally more closely associated with the leaders of the realm. Moreover the Inns were the residence of the intellectual class of the great metropolis; hence they were often called upon to establish the criteria of taste even for the court. In addition, the obligation of the lawyers to entertain the royal family and the nobility required them to display great dramatic diversity and ingenuity in providing such amusement. The Inns of Court were therefore a favorite rendezvous for poets and dramatists.

Classical literature was naturally the repository from which to draw conceptions for the construction of a native drama. As the gentlemen of the Inns of Court knew well this source of inspiration, it is natural that the English imitations of the classical drama which were composed and produced at

called the first English comedy in the English tongue. It is written, not for children, nor to educate, but for grown-ups and solely to delight. It is done into English, not for the vulgar, but for the more advanced taste of the translator's own Inn of Court; it has, therefore, qualities to captivate those who are capable of appreciating high comedy." (By permission of The Macmillan Company, publishers.)

the Inns of Court are somewhat pedantic and "smell too much of that writer Ovid, and that writer Metamorphosis, and talk too much of Proserpina and Jupiter."[43] The Inns and the universities produced, during the sixteenth and seventeenth centuries, a type of drama so distinctive that it is easily distinguishable from the play which was produced in either the public or the private theater: the institutions of learning produced the classical drama, the private theaters the courtly drama, and the public theaters the sensational drama.[44] It is well, on the whole, that the early English play followed an approved form, for two centuries later when it shattered its matrix it proved that it could become greatly disorganized.

The drama as fostered by the Inns of Court has these points in common with the classical drama: it is usually written in blank verse; it ordinarily has five acts; it has paucity of action and heroic speeches; it limits the number of characters appearing on the stage and engaging in dialogue at any one time; it admits of no offensive violence on the stage, though the subject is usually of a sanguinary nature; it ordinarily observes some of the unities of time, place, and action; its characters include the hero, his opponent, Echo, a confidant, a chorus, a messenger, and often a ghost.

The early English play has much in common with the masque: it was frequently written by the composer of the masque; and it originated with the religious play, the foundation of which lies in ritual, while the masque has its origin in the pageant, which, in turn, reverts to the ritual of the agricultural feast, in which the aid of pagan gods was invoked. The characters common to the English classical drama and the masque are the hero and his opponent, Echo, a messenger, and a chorus. The classical play and the English morality play are also similar in that both are rigid in form,

[43] *The Return from Parnassus.*

[44] See Lawrence, pp. 28–29, for a good discussion of this point.

contain stock characters, and are the product of the leisure classes. The development of the various forms of English dramatic entertainment, from mumming to classical drama, may be observed nowhere with greater interest than at the Inns of Court, which fostered practically every type of dramatic entertainment.

The court and the young gentlemen of the Inns, as well as the public generally, eventually tired of a rigid form of exotic entertainment; therefore during the early part of the seventeenth century native comedy was introduced into the play, and even into the masque, by Ben Jonson and others. Thus the similarity between the various types of entertainment became more distinguishable as identical comic characters were introduced into all types.

During the latter part of the seventeenth century, the court seems to have begun to rely less upon the Inns of Court for entertainment than it did in the latter half of the sixteenth century and the early part of the seventeenth. The popularity of the masque and that of tragi-comedy were contemporaneous in London during the first quarter of the seventeenth century. Toward the end of that century, it was only at Oxford that "Shakſpeare and Johnſon had . . . a ſort of claſſical authority," for truly the Inns, with the "metropolitan multitude," had given themselves over to "falſe wit, and forced humour."[45] At this time, diversion at the Inns was provided largely by professional players, who presented dramas which had become popular with the London multitude. Twenty pounds was the usual amount paid for the production of a play, a like sum being paid to the musicians.

Not one of the least important of the dramatic priorities of the Inns of Court in the English drama is collaboration, which later became somewhat common. Literary coöperation,

[45] Chalmers, *Apology*, p. 600.

however, did not originate in England; there is evidence that it existed even in ancient Greece. Nevertheless it was the Inns of Court which introduced dramatic collaboration into England. *Gorboduc*, *Tancred and Gismund*, and *The Misfortunes of Arthur*, all of which were conceived at the Inns of Court or by students of the Inns, were the result of collaboration.

CHAPTER II

Rise of the Inns of Court and Their Internal Organization

THE road to Jerusalem was not an ill setting for the great pageant out of which grew much of the dramatic entertainment of the Inns of Court. The characters of this pageant were fervid Christians who sought solace at the rock-hewn tomb of Jesus. From the early fourth century, with the reputed discovery of the true cross by Helena, mother of Constantine, pilgrimages to the Holy City increased. On the narrow, rocky road leading from the seacoast the lives of the wanderer and his *ménage*, as well as their property, were jeopardized by the Saracen, and often the pilgrim arrived at Jerusalem the less devout because of the loss of his wife or his ox or his talents.

Soon after the appeal of Pope Urban, in 1095, for the protection of the Holy Sepulcher,[1] Hugh Paganus (or de Payens or Pain) of Burgundy, and Godfrey de St. Omer (de St. Audomare) of France, and seven others dedicated themselves to the protection against marauders of travelers to the Holy City. These knights, who were originally Crusaders, having established themselves near the Holy Temple at Jerusalem, called themselves Knights Templars. They adopted as their battle chant "*Non nobis, Domine, non nobis, sed tuo Nomini da gloriam.*" These knights pledged themselves to emulate St. Augustine, and as individuals, but not as an order, to resign riches. Fortunately, Stow[2] has left us an account of the organization of the Knights Templars:

[1] Williamson, p. 4.

[2] John Stow, *The Annales of England* (London, 1592), pp. 193–194.

yr. 1118: About this time, certaine noble men of the horſemen being religiouſly bent, bound themſelves in the hands of the Patriarke of Hieruſalem, to ſerue Chriſt after the manner of regular Chanons, in Chaſtitie, and obedience, and to renounce their owne proper will for euer. Of which order, the firſt was the honourable man Hugh *Paganus*, and *Gawfride de Saint Andemare:* and where at the firſt, they had no certaine habitation, Baldwine king of Hieruſalem graunted them a dwelling place in his pallace by the Temple, and the Chanons of the ſame Temple gaue them the ſtreate thereby to build their houſes of office in, and the Patriarche, the King, the Nobles, and Prelates gaue them certaine reuenues out of their Lordships. Their first poſeſſion was for ſafegarde of the Pilgrims, to keepe the wayes, againſt, the lying in waite of theeues, &c.

About 10. yeeres after, they had a rule appointed them, and a white habit by Pope Honorius, at that time, where they had bene nine in nomber, they began to increaſe into great numbers.

Afterwards in time of Pope Eugenius, they had Croſſes of red cloth ſowed on their uppermoſt garments, to bee knowen from others thereby: and in ſhort, they had their firſt manſion hard by the Temple of our Lorde in Hieruſalem, they were called knightes of the Temple.

The deeds of gallantry of these knights and their imposing entertainment of ambassadors and princes stimulated interest in their cause. In this chivalric age the young nobleman supplanted his lady with Our Lady, and his lord with Our Lord. Temples and monasteries like those at Jerusalem were constructed in all parts of Europe.

The order was probably established in England in 1128, when Hugh Paganus was entertained by Henry I. The first temple, later called the Old Temple, was built in Holborn, or Oldbourne, which was noted for its vineyards. In 1185, at the end of Chancery Lane, a larger building was erected, called the New Temple.

Great military feats, acquisition of wealth, and association with the proudest laity bred arrogance and resultant neglect by the "soldiers of justice" of the purpose for which the order was founded. Of this, Stow says:

> 1241. . . . The Templars in London, at this time in great glory, entertained the nobilitie, foraine Embaſſadors, and the Prince himſelfe very often, inſomuch, that Mathew Paris cryeth out on them for their pride, who being at the firſt ſo poore, as that they had but one horſe to ſerve two of them (in token wherof they gave in their ſeales two men upon one horsebacke) yet sodainely they wared ſo inſolent, that they diſdained other orders, and forced themselues with noble men.[3]

The envy of the common people eventually loosed itself. Factitious charges, with some slight basis in fact, were entered against them, and in 1308, "all the Templars in England were apprehended and committed to priſon in diuers places."[4] Being unable to "purge themſelues" they were, in 1310, "condemned to perpetuall penaunce in ſeueral monaſteries."[5]

The lands of the Templars in Europe included sixteen thousand manors alone. The possessions in England, upon the dissolution of the order, devolved upon the crown. In 1313, Edward II granted the London estates to Thomas, Earl of Lancaster, after whose attainder the New Temple was given to Aimer (Adomar) de Valence, upon whose execution the property reverted to Edward III. Stow says that in 1324, "the landes, lordſhips, and poſſeſſions of the Templars were giuen to the hoſpitallers of Saint John of Jeruſalem, through the whole realme, to be by them poſſeſſed for euer, for the defence of Chriſtendom againſt the Infidels."[6] The hospitalers of St. John soon after granted this property to students of the common law. As, in 1545,[7] "all Colledges, Chauntries, and hoſpitals were committed to the kings order," the law students held directly from the sovereign. During the reign of James I the two temples, with their

[3] John Stow, *The Annales of England* (London, 1592), p. 275.

[4] *Ibid.*, p. 321.

[5] *Ibid.*, p. 324.

[6] *Ibid.*, p. 336.

[7] *Ibid.*, p. 994.

appurtenances, were formally granted to the law students who, because of increase in number, had divided into two bodies called the Society of the Inner Temple and the Society of the Middle Temple,[8] at an annual rental of ten pounds for each society. In the general account books of the Inner Temple appear numerous entries covering payments of this rental.[9]

Gray's Inn, near the end of Chancery Lane, was originally the residence of the lords Gray of Wilton. The prior and convent of Shene later became vested in the title to this property. The convent rented the hostel or Inn to students of the law, who, after dissolution of the convent, rented from the crown. Expenditures for rent often appear in treasurers' accounts of Gray's Inn.[10]

Lincoln's Inn, the fourth of the Inns of Court, was built upon the ruins of the Blackfriars' monastery. Henry Lacy, the Earl of Lincoln, of "the old friar house *juxta* Holborn, being a person well affected to the study of the laws," granted this property to law professors.[11] This Inn appropriately bears the name of the Earl of Lincoln. The property of the bishops of Chichester, which became a part of the estate of the Earl of Lincoln, was granted to law students.

The four Inns of Court rank equally. James Shirley recognized no precedence when he dedicated his masque, *The Triumph of Peace*, to "the four equal and honourable societies of the Inns of Court." The four Inns, each with its subordinate Inns of Chancery, comprised the "judicial university,"[12] analogous to Oxford and Cambridge, with their various colleges.

The internal organization of the Inns of Court is sub-

[8] Formal partition was not made until November, 1732 (Inderwick, Introduction, I).

[9] E.g., Inderwick, III, 115: "For the rent of the House to the Queen's receiver for two years and 2s. for receipts, 20 li. 2s."

[10] November 18, 32 Henry VIII (Herbert, p. 330).

[11] Herbert, p. 289.

[12] Sir William Blackstone.

stantially the same today as it was during the sixteenth and seventeenth centuries. Residents at the Inns were divided into two main groups:

(a) Benchers, or masters of the bench (*Magistri de Banco*), who had jurisdiction over the government of the Inns. As the benchers coöpted new members, they could determine the size of their body.[13] At the Inner and Middle Temples, meetings of the benchers were called parliaments; at Lincoln's Inn, councils; and at Gray's Inn, pensions. During the holiday period, this body ceded its control to the students.[14]

(b) Barristers: the highest office in this division during the latter part of the sixteenth century was the Queen's counsel; next in rank was the sergeant-at-law, and below him the ordinary barrister-at-law.[15] Barristers were of two classes: utter (meaning "complete"; "ouster the bar," meaning "outside the bar") and inner. The utter (or outer) barrister was fully qualified to practice. The inner barrister, originally subordinate to the outer, might, after several years of service as an apprentice or student, become an outer barrister. Today, however, the terms have been reversed, and the utter barrister is now the junior.[16]

The students who, during terms, read the law and attended lectures (readings), were evidently selected with some discrimination. Those admitted were almost always of wealthy, ranking families. Admission was usually by payment of a sum of money or the equivalent.[17] In the records of some of the Inns the students are often infantilely designated "pro" or "pa" (perhaps to distinguish them as Protestant or Papist), or "very lerned," "of gret lyvine," "welthy," "of

[13] Williamson, p. 108.

[14] Bedwell, p. 69.

[15] Dillon, p. 12.

[16] Graham, p. 570; also Inderwick, Introduction, I, xxxii.

[17] Brian Tuke was excused of all other charges because he agreed to contribute to a projected sea-wall, and Richard Stapleton because he donated a "pipe of wine to the value of 46s. 8d" (Inderwick, I, 75 and 106, respectively).

gret practise," and the like.[18] Appendix A of this volume contains a survey of chambers and students at the Inns of Court in 1574. The following rambling account of Fortescue may give some conception of the nature of the student body:[19]

> The only way they have of punishing the delinquents, is by expelling them the society: which punishment they dread more than criminals do imprisonment and irons: for he who is expelled out of one society, is never taken in by any of the other. Whence it happens, that there is a constant harmony amongst them, the greatest friendship and a general freedom of conversation. I need not be particular in describing the manner and method how the laws are studied in those places, since your Highness[20] is never like to be a student there. But, I may say in the general, that it is pleasant, excellently well adapted for proficiency, and every way worthy of your esteem and encouragement. One thing more I will beg leave to observe, that neither at *Orleans*, where both the *Canon* and *Civil Laws* are professed and studied; and whither students resort from all parts; neither at *Angiers*, *Caen*, nor any other University in *France* (*Paris* excepted) are there so many students, who have past their minority, as in our *Inns of Court*, where the natives only are admitted. . . . Great caution seems formerly to have been observed in admitting persons as members of the Inns of Court, whose rank in society, and whose education was not a guarantee for the propriety of their conduct. There is extant an order of King James, signed by Sir E. Coke, Lord Bacon and others, that none but gentlemen by descent should be received.

The governing body of the Inner Temple was essentially like that of the other Inns. Therefore the officers comprising this body at the Inner Temple will be used as criteria:

The chief officer, elected annually from the benchers, was the treasurer (*Thesaurarius*).[21] He had control of the receipts and disbursements of the Inn, and rendered an annual

18 Inderwick, Introduction, I, lxxix.
19 *De Laudibus Legum Angliae*, pp. 186–187.
20 This work was written for the instruction of the young Prince Edward.
21 Williamson, p. 108.

account thereof; he had jurisdiction over the maintenance of the buildings, and presided over the parliaments.[22]

During the early sixteenth century three governors were selected from the benchers to assist the treasurer; these offices, however, no longer exist.[23]

Two annual nominations were made to the office of reader (*Lector*): one for the Lent reading (*Quadragesima*) and another for the summer (*Autumnalia*) reading. Eligibility to the Lent readership necessitated previous service in the summer readership, but the summer reader might not have held previously the office of reader. Elections to readerships were made from the outer barristers. After expiration of his term of service the reader was entitled, in due course, to election as master of the bench. The reader was required to deliver readings or lectures on assigned legal subjects. Some of these readings, such as Bacon on the Statute of Uses, Treherne on the Forest Laws, and Callis on Sewers, have become legal masterpieces.[24] The reader also presided over the moots; in addition, he had the right to call to the bar.[25] Each reader was required to provide a feast, called the reader's feast, for all the members of the Inn. This office consequently entailed considerable expense, but declination of office involved a penalty, fixed at £40 in 1547,[26] and the possibility of expulsion from service as a master of the bench.

Four auditors, two selected from the benchers and two from the bar, audited the annual accounts of the treasurer. After the audit, these officers gave an elaborate dinner at the expense of the Inn. A pensioner collected and accounted for the pensions owing to the Inn.

The English fondness for putting one in one's place is nowhere better exemplified than in the seating in the great

[22] Williamson, p. 108; Bellot, *The Inner and Middle Temple,* p. 37; Inderwick, Introduction, I, xxxii.

[23] Bellot, p. 37.

[24] Inderwick, Introduction, I, xxxii.

[25] Bedwell, p. 200.

[26] Bellot, p. 37.

hall of the Inner Temple. The long table across the hall was used by the treasurer, the reader, the masters, and distinguished guests; another table was assigned to the utter barristers, a third to the inner barristers, a fourth to the "clerks commoner," often admitted from the Inns of Chancery. Behind a screen was a fifth table, occupied by the benchers' clerks. In addition, separate tables were often provided for undistinguished guests, like singers.

Perfect harmony seems to have existed between the various houses. In 1667–68, however, ambassadors of the Middle Temple offered an affront to the Inner Temple, but after apology the "ancient amity" was "renewed and continued";[27] some time before, during the reign of Elizabeth, it is asserted that the Middle Temple endeavored to obtain Lyon's Inn of Chancery from the Inner Temple, but the bond of friendship which existed between Gray's Inn and the Inner Temple proved too strong for the Middle Temple.[28]

As has already been said, the legal profession in England is a product of the guild system. Master lawyers, at first through voluntary association, formed a close organization for practice in the courts; this union contemplated the exclusion of unqualified practitioners and direction of the study of the law. Behind the guild system, that did much to mold and to make uniform the laws of England, are the monastic institutions, which transmitted the ancient laws of England, as well as the civil and canonic laws of Rome. King Stephen's prohibition of the study of the laws imported from Italy, which was considered an act of impiety, created much agitation in ecclesiastical institutions. However, long before the reign of Stephen, the laws of the South, and particularly the ecclesiastical laws, had become so fused with the civil laws of the North that no act of sovereignty could sever them. The law has ever been the shadow of man's philosophy. As phi-

[27] Inderwick, III, 56.

[28] Pitt-Lewis, pp. 74–75.

losophy changes, its shadow, the law, is reflected behind it; sometimes, of course, the servile shadow assumes such grotesque shapes that it seems to be caricaturing its master. But real change in the law can be accomplished only by mutation in the concepts of life. As man introduces new gods into the state, his law tends to conform. Man's religion, then, underlies his law. It is peculiarly interesting that, in addition to the blending of ecclesiastical and civil law, as it is found in England, the English legal system was nurtured in the very houses which fostered and protected Christianity, and that customs of the training schools in the law rest heavily upon monastic tradition. One especially interesting survival is the Inner Temple Grace Book, written in two hands, containing many graces no longer used.[29] At the Inner Temple remain the cloisters, the chapels, the refectory, the library, the buttery, the brewery, the great hall, the graveyard, and the gardens, much as they were when the original Templars inhabited them.

Study of the laws was not the sole object of residence at the Inns. Dugdale[30] tells us that

> the Students in them, did there, not only ſtudy the Laws, but uſe such other exerciſes as might make them the more ſerviceable to the King's Court. . . . So that theſe Hostells being Nurſeries or Seminaries of the Court, taking their denomination of the end wherefore they were ſo inſtituted, were called therefore the Innes of Court.

Law students then were the *arrière-ban* of the crown; their function, like that of the Knights Templars, was partly military. With pride and with propriety they sometimes assumed the appellation of their predecessors, "soldiers of justice," and in every war they have proved themselves worthy of this designation.

At sunset "a general light collation might be allowed and

[29] Inderwick, III, Appendix IV. [30] *Origines Juridiciales*, p. 141.

wine partaken of"[31] by the Knights Templars, and so we find records of many intra- and inter-Inn potations. On March 14, 20 Henry VI (1442), "Richard Wode received from the Treasurer . . . 49s. 5d. for a drinking bout . . . between Lincoln's Inn and the Middle Temple."[32]

The Knights Templars were allowed to dress in black or brown (*burrel*) only; and any brother desiring the best or finest garments was to be given the worst.[33] Similarly, members of the Middle Temple and of Lincoln's Inn were forbidden to wear "great bryches in their hoses," upon pain of fine or expulsion; nor were they allowed to wear "any gownes, but such as were of a sad colour."[34]

The Templars were required to "keep their hair and beards trimmed with regularity so that there should be neither superfluity nor eccentricity (*facetiae vitium*)."[35] Likewise, the gentlemen of the Middle Temple and of Lincoln's Inn were forbidden to have "long or curled hayr."[36]

The conventual regulations required that what the Templars did not eat should be given to the servants or "to the poor in brotherly charity."[37] The Inner Temple regulations provided that "all broken bread and drink, with the chippings, be only and wholly employed to the use of the poor,"[38] and again, that the poor should be "served before five of the clock in the cloister, in times of health, and in the garden in time of sickness, under the pain of 2s."[39]

The rules of the monastery provided also that "No sisters

[31] Williamson, p. 14, quoting Article 16 of Council of Troyes of 1128.

[32] Inderwick, Introduction, I, xvi, quoting Black Book of Lincoln's Inn, I, fol. 44d.

[33] Williamson, pp. 14–15, quoting Articles 20–22 and 25 of Council of Troyes of 1128.

[34] Herbert, pp. 242 and 311–317, quoting Orders for Government, 4 and 5 Ph. & M.

[35] Williamson, p. 15, quoting Articles 28–29 of Council of Troyes of 1128.

[36] Herbert, pp. 242 and 311–317.

[37] Williamson, p. 14, quoting Article 14 of Council of Troyes of 1128.

[38] Inderwick, I, 341.

[39] *Ibid.*, II, 25.

were to be admitted, because the ancient enemy of souls, through the society of women, has driven many from the straight path to Paradise (*expulit a recto tramite paradisi*)."[40] Similarly, women were excluded from the gentlemen's chambers at the Inns of Court; even laundresses must have reached the discretionary age of forty before they might be admitted.[41] The Inner Temple regulation, which, by its own terms almost invites violation, is, nevertheless, very explicit:

> Item, that no woman shall have recourse to the gentlemen's chambers for any cause, except to be as suitors to "experyensors" in term times, openly, without evil suspect, upon pain of forfeiture of 3s. 4d. for every time any such woman shall have resort, the same to be paid by the gentleman that lieth in the chamber whereunto any such resort shall be found or perceived.[42]

The precepts of the Knights Templars which were adopted by the gentlemen of the Inns of Court are infinite.

As the Inns were institutions for the training of the wealthier classes (*apprenticii nobiliores*) the curriculum included whatever conduced to a liberal education. The gentlemen were taught music,[43] and dancing,[44] and military tactics. The Inns also patronized the drama. They were often the scene of splendid banquets and entertainments, to which the sovereign was invited, just as in the heyday of the Knights Templars. The great halls of the Inns were the natural places for grand gatherings, for they were nearly as large as any in the realm.[45] According to tradition, while Eliza-

[40] Williamson, p. 15, quoting Article 56 of the Council of Troyes of 1128.

[41] Inderwick, *seriatim;* and Herbert, p. 335, *et seq.*

[42] Inderwick, I, 162.

[43] "William Saunders, the head of the musicians of the inn, was a person of acknowledged merit. After the restoration, he petitioned the king for a place in the band of royal violins," which he obtained (Inderwick, II, cxxviii).

[44] Account of Treasurer, February 27, 1653–54, Middle Temple Records: "Dancers and others, gratuity for instructing the gentlemen . . . £20."

[45] The "re-edifying" of Gray's Inn hall cost £4,000; it is 75′ × 35′ × 47′ high. An elaborate oak screen separating an anteroom from the main hall is supposed to be the gift of Elizabeth (Bellot, pp. 6–7).

beth was being entertained at one of the Inns, she so much enchanted two of the students that they, because of her unapproachableness, resolved to put themselves to death. At any rate, the relationship between the sovereign and the Inns was always friendly, and the opinion of the gentlemen of the Inns seems to have been of some weight with the crown. In February, 1681–82, several gentlemen of Gray's Inn presented "declarations . . . to his majestie . . . testifying their abhorrence of all trayterous associations."[46]

One of the best descriptions of the Inns of Court is that of Fortescue,[47] who says:

> In these greater inns a student cannot well be maintained under *eight and twenty pounds* a year: and, if he have a servant to wait on him (as for the most part they have) the expence is proportionably more: for this reason, the students are sons to persons of quality; those of an inferior rank not being able to bear the expences of maintaining and educating their children in this way. As to the merchants, they seldom care to lessen their stock in trade by being at such large yearly expences. So that there is scarce to be found, throughout the kingdom, an eminent lawyer, who is not a gentleman by birth and fortune; *consequently they have a greater regard for their character and honour than those who are bred in another way.* There is both in the *Inns of Court*, and the *Inns of Chancery*, a sort of an *Academy*, or *Gymnasium*, fit for persons of their station; where they learn singing, and all kinds of music, dancing and such other accomplishments and diversions (which are called *Revels*) as are suitable to their quality, and such as are usually practised at Court. At other times, out of term, the greater part apply themselves to the study of the law. Upon festival days, and after the offices of the church are over, they employ themselves in the study of sacred and prophane history: here every thing which is good and virtuous is to be learned: all vice is discouraged and banished. So that knights, barons, and the greatest nobility of the kingdom, often place their children in those Inns of Court; not so much to make the laws their

[46] Luttrell, p. 167.
[47] *De Laudibus Legum Angliae*, pp. 183–188.

study, much less to live by the profession (having large patrimonies of their own) but to form their manners and to preserve them from the contagion of vice. The discipline is so excellent, that there is scarce ever known to be any picques or differences, any bickerings or disturbances amongst them.

Another interesting description by a foreigner, that of Paul Hentzner,[48] a German who made a tour of England in 1598, follows:

There are 15 colleges within and without the city (London), nobly built with beautiful gardens adjoining. Of these the three principal are:

I. The Temple (*Templum vulgo Tempel*),
II. Gray's Inn (Grezin), and
III. Lincolns Inn (Lynconsin).

In these colleges, numbers of the young nobility, gentry and others are educated and chiefly in the Study of Physics, for very few apply themselves to that of the law: (*Philosophiae, theologiae et medicinae potissimum operam dantes*). They are allowed a very good table, and silver cups[49] to drink out of. Once a person of distinction who could not help being surprised at the great number of silver cups said "He should have thought it more suitable to the life of students if they had used rather glass or earthenware than silver." The College answered, "They were ready to make him a present of all their plate provided he would undertake to supply them with all the glass and earthenware they should have a demand for; since it was very likely he would find the expence, from constant breaking, exceed the value of the silver."

It was not until about 1700 that the residents of the Inns began to devote themselves with great seriousness to the study of the law; theretofore, the pursuit of one's inclination was the chief aim. Good fellowship was, however, always in the ascendant. Ordinarily, as became their rank and

[48] *A Journey into England in the year MDXCVIII*, p. 29.

[49] In most of the Inns, as records of purchase indicate, green pots were used.

age,[50] the students were dignified; but sometimes the gaiety and buoyancy of youth found expression in pranks that approached the unmannerly. The firing of arms in the Inner Temple necessitated the following regulation: "Shooters with guns within this House to forfeit, videlicet, for every shot, the master 20s. and the man 10s."[51] Perhaps it was the outcome of a legal argument which an unorthographical, but ingenuous secretary recorded as follows: "Richard Clerk amerced 20s. because he shamefully called out divers opprobrious words within the hall of the Temple to John Hylham, of the society, saying and calling out that the same John was a 'hourson knave.' "[52] Sometimes the young gentlemen became frolicsome at the table, and threw bread or broke steins in their zeal to be served. The following entry was probably meant in no way to disparage the service at Gray's Inn: "It is ordered that gents shall forbeare throwing of bread and breaking of potts and shall sitt quietly in the hall at their tables and be messed as the servants bring upp their meate."[53] Occasionally the students raided the brewery; at one time they consumed surreptitiously—however that may have been done—thirty-two barrels of beer,[54] and, at another time, bread was "embezzled out of the buttery."[55]

The Inns were, in many ways, the most colorful places in all London. During the plague, many strangers, "to the great annoyance of the students,"[56] established themselves in the Inns. Numerous dissolute persons, because the Temple was originally a place of sanctuary, secreted themselves in the chambers. The presence of these strangers, as well as some who were there by invitation, was, of course, prejudicial to the morality of the students, who, without such contacts, had

[50] The Inns were, in one sense, postgraduate institutions. Many of the students had been graduated from Oxford or Cambridge. The common age at the Inns was somewhat more than twenty-one.

[51] Inderwick, I, 234.

[52] *Ibid.*, p. 89.

[53] Fletcher, I, January 30, 1621.

[54] Inderwick, III, 282.

[55] *Ibid.*

[56] *Ibid.*, I, 284.

sufficient disposition to debauchery. In the Inner Temple, in 1581, criminal persons became so annoying that the gardener's men and the under-cooks were designated to make "privy searches within the precincts of this House for rogues, and help carry them to Bridewell or to some other place of punishment."[57] It was these fugitives from justice who, sometimes in collusion with the servants, stole the pewter and silver that was in use and on display on feast days.[58] Expenditures were often made to reimburse pewterers for losses of rented service.[59]

Every few months some incident ruffled the routine at the Inns. In 1649, Mr. Thorpe became "crazie in his wits, and a nuisance to . . . his chamber fellow."[60] John Chamberlain wrote to Sir Dudley Carlton that

> Maxwell, a sewer or gentleman-usher . . . plucked or pinched one Hawley, a gentleman of the Temple, by the ear . . . that the blood flowed fastly . . . the matter came to the King's notice; he, understanding that all the inns of court took alarm at the abuses, . . . told them that . . . he would hear the matter himself.[61]

In another letter Chamberlain told Sir Dudley that Sir John Tyndall, a master of the Chancery, was killed in Lincoln's Inn by one of his clients.[62]

During the sixteenth and seventeenth centuries, the Inns of Court were much like the rest of London: beauty was mingled with much of the foulness of the earth. The records of the Inns bristle with pictures of the glory and of the

[57] Inderwick, I, 317.

[58] In the early eighteenth century, the plate for service at Gray's Inn consisted of "one basin, a ewer, a goblet, four candlesticks, two great salts and one little salt, twelve forks, sixteen spoons, one masteth [possibly a punch bowl], two tankards, two bowls with covers, two salvers, and one pair of snuffers with box" (Bellot, pp. 36–38).

[59] E.g., Inderwick, I, 278, II, 81, III, 328–329; Black Book, II, 102.

[60] Hopwood, I, 79.

[61] Birch, *C. & T. of James*, I, 166–167.

[62] *Ibid.*, p. 437.

degradation of the times. They reveal the fact that the young lawyer was meticulously indifferent to sanitation: it was found necessary at Gray's Inn even to forbid the casting of "Afhes, Filth, or Dirt" into the courts from the windows.[63] In 1658, at the Inner Temple, a lighterman was paid 9*s*. 4*d*. for "carrying out half the rubbish in the churchyard,"[64] and, in the following year, Smith, the lighterman, was given 12*s*. for "carrying away 48 tons of rubbish out of the garden."[65] At the same Inn, a "rat catcher" was paid 2*s*. 6*d*. "for killing the rats and mice in the hall against the summer reading, by Mr. Reader's commandment."[66] While it appears that much preparation was made to have the Inns appear at their best during entertainment periods, yet there was at each of the Inns a force of servants assigned to cleaning and sweeping. For instance, William Knight, a glover, was permitted to keep a shop "under the Gate" of the Inner Temple, with the provision that he should keep "the place about the shop clean and sweet," and that he should, further, give annually to the treasurer a pair of gloves.[67] In the cloisters of the Inner Temple, many persons maintained shops without warrant; so that an order of expulsion had to be adopted.[68] In the crypt or ambulatory of Lincoln's Inn, barristers conferred with their clients, and students argued on the merits of the cases which they studied. This ambulatory, like the cloisters of the Temple, was the scene of amorous *liaisons* at night.[69]

Not one of the least items of expenditure at the Temple is that for the maintenance of children abandoned there. To suggest that these foundlings resulted from extra-connubial peccadilloes of the students might be unjustified. However, Mr. Richard D'Ewes, a student of the law, had some difficulty in disproving paternity of one of the children aban-

[63] Dugdale, p. 291.
[64] Inderwick, II, 331.
[65] *Ibid.*, p. 336.
[66] *Ibid.*, p. 92.
[67] *Ibid.*, Introduction, I, lxxv.
[68] *Ibid.*, II, 449.
[69] Heckethorn, p. 27.

doned at the steps.[70] The ancient right of sanctuary, which was invoked by many who were "heavy laden," may account for the numerous desertions at the Temple. The children were "farmed out" at an annual expense of about three pounds for each infant. As the number of abandonments increased, the financial burden to the Inns became almost intolerable.[71] Therefore, in 1699, we find that the Inner Temple, in a most un-Solomonic manner, paid "Dry and the under-porter" ten shillings "for pursuit after a woman that dropped a child and fixing the child upon her."[72] More often than not, the abandoned child died, involving expense of burial by the Inns. Numerous allowances were made for "graves-diggin for . . . nurse children"[73] and for conduct of the funeral.[74] The foundlings were often given the family name "Temple." During the fiscal year 1695–96 of the Inner Temple are recorded expenditures for the illness and burial of Christmas Temple, evidently abandoned, ironically enough, during the holiday season.[75]

On the whole, the students were extraordinarily generous to painstaking employes. Only the careless, like John Coke, who was amerced ten shillings for being "negligent and wasteful in spices and other things of the society,"[76] were punished. The records indicate that no objection was ever made to increasing the salary of conscientious employes. During the plague and periods of dearth, special provision was made for their comfort. As examples of the charity of the Inner Temple, the Widow "Fridaysweed" Crow was granted one pound for the relief of her son, "Pennifeather" Crow,

[70] Hopwood, I, 73.

[71] In 1696, the Under-treasurer of the Inner Temple was ordered to "give an account of the bastards kept by the House" (Inderwick, III, 328).

[72] *Ibid.*, p. 351.

[73] *Ibid.*, p. 90.

[74] *Ibid.*, II, 110, 232, 274.

[75] *Ibid.*, III, 328–329. Seventeen other Temples were provided for.

[76] Inner Temple Records, Parliament, February 7, 1520–21.

a sick servant, and another pound for his burial;[77] and the expense of interment of a stranger, found dead on the steps of the Temple, was borne by the same students.[78] Richard Robinson, whose lute was broken at the Inner Temple, was fully indemnified;[79] a collection was taken for the destitute queen of Bohemia, who, as Princess Elizabeth, had been entertained at the Inner Temple;[80] and twenty pounds was granted to Oxford University for the repair of its schools.[81] Lincoln's Inn resolved to have no reveling on Purification day in 1678 because of the recent "dreadful fire" at the Temple.[82] Gray's Inn subscribed a hundred guineas for the comfort of the English troops at Boston during the American Revolution.[83]

The Inns of Court were truly

> . . . an awful chaos—light and darkness,
> And mind and dust, and passions and pure thoughts
> Mix'd.[84]

[77] Inderwick, III, 320.
[78] *Ibid.*, II, 110.
[79] *Ibid.*, p. 321.
[80] *Ibid.*, Introduction, II, cxxix.
[81] *Ibid.*, II, 92.
[82] Melmoth, Appendix, pp. 344–345.
[83] Bellot, p. 18.
[84] Byron's "Manfred," III–I.

CHAPTER III

Professional Revels

A. THE READER'S FEAST

AMONG the most pretentious of the professional revels were the readings during Lent. Another rather important annual feast heretofore noted was that given after the audit of the treasurer's accounts.[1] Moots (probably from the Anglo-Saxon *mot,* meeting, rather than from the French *mot,* as has been said often) were sometimes held by the seniors during the reading period. They were formal arguments by students of the law on theoretical cases,[2] and were held in the hall, which was arranged as a courtroom. Boltings (perhaps from *bolter,* sieve: a sifting of cases), similar exercises by juniors, consisted of presentation of various cases and arguments upon their merits. Moots and boltings were sometimes followed by revelry[3] of the students.

At the feasts, which were a part of the readings, noblemen, ambassadors, and sometimes the sovereign, were entertained. In 1615–16, at the Middle Temple reading, the guests of honor were the French, Venetian, Savoyard, and States' ambassadors.[4] The readership, being an office of great distinction, involved the expenditure of tremendous sums, often as much

[1] From Inner Temple Records: "To Chilton, for wine for the House and for the supper of the auditors of the treasurer's account, 19 li. 4s. 3d." and "For the supper at the treasurer's accounts 1626, 6li. 4s. 6d. (Inderwick, III, 16, and I, 165, respectively).

[2] In the modern law school, participation in moot, or practice, court, is a part of the curriculum.

[3] This entertainment may be compared to the annual "spread" at the New England universities.

[4] Nichols, *James,* III, 131. In 1668, Evelyn attended the reading feast at the Middle Temple, "a pompous entertainment, where were the Archbishop of Canterbury, and all great Earls and Lords" (August 4).

as a thousand pounds in three weeks. The Lent reader usually entered on his reading on the first Monday in Lent. For several days preceding, he secluded himself in his chamber, not appearing at commons even, in order that his first appearance might be the more splendid because of his previous absence. On Sunday afternoon, however, accompanied by the benchers, with two ranking readers as his assistants, he attended church, with a richly liveried retinue of more than a dozen servants. On Sunday afternoon, very grandiosely, he entered the great hall, where he took supper at the head of the benchers' table.

On the following morning, after breakfast in the parliament room, he formally delivered his books and papers to the assistant lecturer. After the reader took the oath of allegiance, his assistant read the statute on the subject which was to be expounded. Then, very gravely, the reader began his lecture, minimizing his knowledge of the subject and apologizing for his legal frailties.

Judges and sergeants who had been nurtured in the house attended in their purple robes and scarlet hoods. One was duly impressed with their superiority by the fact that they were seated with their backs to the speaker.

The reading was concluded with a grand feast at the expense of the reader; at this time, even the subordinates were honored with an "extraordinary dish."

During three days in the week, Monday, Wednesday, and Friday, for three weeks[5] this lecture method was followed, the other days being spent in banqueting and entertaining notable persons.[6] Charles II, with his suite, was a guest at the reading of Sir Francis Goodricke, in February, 1671–72, at Lincoln's Inn.[7]

[5] These readings originally continued for a month; the time was later reduced to three weeks; and then to a fortnight (Herbert, p. 237).

[6] Herbert, pp. 232, *et seq.*

[7] See reproduction of autographs of this party.

It was the duty of the chief butler to provide a "white Rod, and a white ſtaff for the Readers elect."[8] Students were assigned to the duty of carrying meat to the reader's table. After the readings were completed, the students accompanied the reader to his residence with much formality; in the evening they invited him to be their guest at dinner.

After his reading, he became a bencher; at the first meeting of the parliament, the merits of the reader were expatiated upon, and, after fulsome compliments by him to the society, he might, in a weak voice, becoming a person in the lowest seat, cast his vote.

Upon being called to the bench table, the reader elect gave a "garnish of wine" for his own welcome, and, when he was removed to the "auncients' table," he was similarly honored.[9]

Sometimes the reader served twice, in which case he was called a "double reader."

At the reader's feast,[10] one of the readers placed in an orderly fashion on the table all the service which had been brought to him by the students; the other reader attended the prominent guests. During the feast, both of these officers curtsied in approved solemn manner to the judges and sergeants. While the hall was being cleared after the feast, the readers elect entertained in the garden; in a short while, they returned to the hall, where the ancient, or superior, reader,[11] with a white staff in his hand, placed himself before the bar table; the puisne reader[12] with a white rod in his hand, took his station at the cupboard, where, after the music began, he called the master of the revels twice;[13] with decorum, the ancient disdained the first call; but, at the second, he ad-

[8] Dugdale, p. 200. [9] Herbert, p. 231.

[10] The reader originally gave a dinner and a supper or drinking (Black Books, Preface, II).

[11] The master of the revels. [12] The master of ceremonies.

[13] In some of the Inns, he called three times.

These autographs are reproduced from the plate engraved for the fourth edition of Lane's "Student's Guide through Lincoln's Inn," 1823.

AUTOGRAPHS OF ILLUSTRIOUS PERSONAGES ENTERTAINED AT LINCOLN'S INN HALL ON FEBRUARY 29, 1671

vanced, leading the measures, followed by the other gentlemen in order of precedence. The description of Dugdale[14] of the entertainment at the reader's feast is of sufficient importance and interest to warrant its being quoted:

When the laſt meaſure is dancing, the Reader at the Cupboard, calls to one of the Gentlemen of the Bar, as he is walking or dancing with the reſt, to give the Judges a Song: who forthwith begins the firſt line of any Pſalm, as he thinks fitteſt; after which, all the reſt of the Company follow, and ſing with him. Whileſt they are thus walking and ſinging, the Reader with the white Rod, departs from the Cup-board, and makes his choice of a competent number of Utter-Bariſters, and as many under the Bar, whom he takes into the Buttry; where, there is delivered unto every Bariſter, a Towel with wafers in it; and unto every Gentleman under the Barr, a wooden Bowl, filled with Ipocras,[15] with which they march in order into the Hall, the Reader with his white Rod, going foremoſt. And when they come near to the half pace, oppoſite to the Judges, the Company divide themſelves, one half (as well Bariſters, as thoſe under the Bar) ſtanding on the one ſide of the Reader; the other on the other ſide: and then, after a low ſolemn Congee made, the Gentlemen of the Bar firſt carry the Wafers; the reſt, with the new Reader, ſtanding in their places. At their return, they all make another ſolemn low Congee, and then the Gentlemen under the Bar, carry their Bowls of Ipocras to the Judges: and returning, when the Judges have drank, they make the like ſolemn Congee, and ſo all depart, ſaving the new Readers elect, who wait upon the Judges untill their departure; and then uſher them down the Hall, unto the Court Gate, where they take their leaves of them.

In the ſelf ſame manner, they entertain the Judges and Serjeants on All-Hallown day and on the Feaſt day of the Purification of our Lady. Which two Feaſts, viz. All Saints and Candlemaſs, are the onely Feaſts in the whole year, made purpoſely for the Judges and Sergeants in this Society: but of later time, divers Noblemen have been mixed with them, and ſolemnly invited as Gueſts to the Din-

[14] *Origines Juridiciales,* pp. 205, *et seq.*, the Middle Temple.

[15] A drink, which legend says was strained through the sleeve of Hippocrates.

ner, in regard they were formerly of the Society. . . . (Befides thefe folemn Revels or meafures aforefaid, they had wont to be entertained with Poft Revels, performed by the better fort of the young Gentlemen of the Society with Galliards, Corrantoes, and other Dances; or elfe with Stage-playes: the firft of thefe Feafts being at the beginning, and the other at the later end of Chriftmas. But of late years, thefe Poft Revells have been difufed, both here and in the other Innes of Court. . . .) This Courfe he obferves three dayes in a week, untill the end of the Reading, viz. every Munday, Wednefday, and Fryday, the other intermediate dayes being fpent in Feafting, and entertainment of Strangers, who are commonly great Lords and other eminent perfons: but, be the Guefts of never fo high a degree, the Reader, within the Precincts of the Houfe, hath precedence of them: and at the Table keeps his Chair at the upper end. His expences during this time of Reading, are very great; infomuch as fome have fpent about fix hundred pounds in two dayes lefs then a fortnight, which now is the ufual time of Reading, . . . there being few Summer Readers, who, in half the time that heretofore a Reading was wont to continue, fpent so little as threefcore Bucks, befides Red Deer: fome have fpent fourfcore, fome an hundred; whereof one brace of Bucks are commonly beftowed on New Inne, to feaft the Students there: And the neighbour Parifhes to the Temple, do alfo tafte of the Reader's bounty in this kind. Yet fome help the Reader hath from the Houfe, which allows every fingle Reader, One Hogfhead of Wine,[16] or five pounds in money; and a fpecial admittance of any Gentleman into the Houfe, or five pounds more in lieu thereof. Befides, in the laft week of his Reading, a great and coftly Feaft is provided for the entertainment of foreign Ambaffadours, Earls, Lords, and men of eminent quality: which although it be call'd the Readers Feaft, yet he bears no part of the chardge, the fame being impofed on four gentlemen of the Houfe.[17] The Reader ufed to be Steward of the houfe for the time of Chriftmas, but now he is relieved, paying a reafonable Fine for the fame: the which Fine is now turned into a

[16] This allowance was later increased.

[17] This statement is not entirely correct; as the reader sometimes entertained his own guests at the feast, he often bore a part of the expenses.

Brawn and Mufkadine, which the Summer Reader doth beftow on the Gentlemen of the Houfe.

Perhaps the most famous reader's feast at the Inner Temple was that held on Thursday, August 15, 1661, by Sir Heneage Finch, which was attended by the king and the dukes of York, Buckingham, Richmond, and Ormond. The royal party, which sailed on the river from Whitehall, was met at the Temple stairs by Sir Heneage and Sir Orlando Bridgman, lord chief justice of the common pleas, the latter attired in scarlet robe. On the side of the walk to the Temple garden were alined the reader's servants in white tabba doublets;[18] continuing this formation were the benchers and the barristers, clad in gowns. Twenty violins were played during the entire visit of the king. Dinner was served by fifty gowned gentlemen. The king and the Duke of York sat at a table on a dais at the upper end of the hall; the noblemen sat on the right side of the hall, and the reader and the gentlemen of the society on the left.[19]

The chief biographer of Francis North[20] has left an interesting account of the reading of the lord keeper at the Middle Temple:

During his solicitorship, his lordship kept his public reading in the Temple hall, in the autumnal vacation. . . . He took for his subject the statute of fines, and, under that, found means to exhaust all his learning upon that branch of the law which concerned titles, and the transferring them: and the arguers against him did their parts also, who were the best lawyers of the society in that time. As for the feasting part it was sumptuous, and, in three or four days time, cost one thousand pounds at least. The grandees of the court dined there, and of the quality (as they call it) enough; for his diffused relation, general acquaintance, and station, as well as pros-

[18] The reader furnished the livery for the servants.

[19] Dugdale, pp. 157–158; Herbert, p. 203; Inderwick, Introduction, III, x.

[20] *The Life of the Right Honourable Francis North, Baron of Guilford, Lord Keeper of the Great Seal, etc.*, by the Hon. Roger North, pp. 149–151.

pect of his advancing in the king's service, made a great rendezvous of all the better sort, then in town, at his feasts.

He sent out the officers with white staves (for so the way was) and a long list to invite; but he went himself to wait upon the archbishop of Canterbury, Sheldon; for so also the ceremony required. The archbishop received him very honourably, and would not part with him at the stair's head, but, telling him he was no ordinary reader, went down, and did not part till he saw him pass at his outward gate. I cannot much commend the extravagance of the feasting used at these readings; and that of his lordship's was so terrible an example, that I think none hath ventured since to read publicly; but the exercise is turned into a revenue, and a composition is paid into the treasury of the society. Therefore one may say, as was said of Cleomenes, that, in this respect, his lordship was *ultimus heroum*, the last of the heroes. And the profusion of the best provisions and wine was to the worst of purposes, debauchery, disorder, tumult, and waste.[21] I will give but one instance; upon the grand day, as it was called, a banquet was provided to be set upon the table, composed of pyramids, and smaller services in form. The first pyramid was at least four feet high, with stages one above another. The conveying this up to the table, through a crowd, that were in full purpose to overturn it, was no small work: but, with the friendly assistance of the gentlemen, it was set whole upon the table. But, after it was looked upon a little, all went, hand over head, among the rout in the hall, and, for the more part, was trod under foot. The entertainment, the nobility had out of this, was, after they had tossed away the dishes, a view of the crowd in confusion, wallowing over one another, and contending for a dirty share of it.

It may be said this was for want of order; but, in truth, it was for want of a regular and disciplined guard of soldiers; for nothing less would keep order there. I do not think it was a just regulation, when, for the abuse, they took away such a profitable exercise. . . . It was the design of these readers to explain to the students the con-

[21] North probably disliked this, because once while a youth, he, drunk, fell from his horse; and, at another time, he barely escaped death in a pond, after having been with "one of the greatest kill-cows at drinking in the nation" (*The Life of the Right Honourable Francis North, Baron of Guilford, Lord Keeper of the Great Seal, etc.*, pp. 88–89).

structions that were to be made upon new statutes, for clearing a way that counsel might advise safely upon them.

In 1677 occurred the last reading at Gray's Inn.[22]

For a long while, it was thought that the expense at the reader's feast was exorbitant. As early as 1513, sumptuary regulation was found necessary at the Middle Temple, where, in preparation for the feast, numerous bucks were being received. The number was then limited to twelve,[23] but it was gradually increased to thirty.[24] It is said that the summer reader had often provided as many as eighty or a hundred bucks, which, considering the number of guests, was not great. At Gray's Inn, it was provided, in 1591, that the reader should be limited to two hogsheads of wine.[25] The alarm of the Inner Temple is revealed in the following act of parliament:

> Whereas grand readings in the Inns of Court . . . never intended that the readers should . . . be put unto such great and excessive cost and charges in unnecessary feasting and entertainments, . . . be it therefore enacted . . . that . . . no reader . . . shall come into the hall . . . in order to keep any supper, except it be for the first day when the reader is to take his place in the hall.[26]

In the sixteenth year of the reign of Charles II (1676), it was provided that "no Reader have above twelve attendants in Liveries, nor exceed above three hundred pounds in the whole charge of his Reading, except ſuch as are of the Kings, Queens, or Princes Councell, etc."[27] In 1678 an agreement limiting the expenses attendant upon readings was arrived at among the four Inns: the pension at Gray's provided:

> Whereas his Matie hath signified his pleasure That noe reader . . . should expend above three hundred pounds . . . it is agreed by general consent of the 4 inns of court as followeth:

[22] Fletcher, II, Introduction, ix.
[23] Middle Temple Records, p. 42, July 4, 1513.
[24] Williamson, p. 131.
[25] Fletcher, I, 91.
[26] Inderwick, III, 6.
[27] Pitt-Lewis, p. 29.

1st that noe Reader do give livery to any above the number of two and that to attend his person.

2ly that noe publique entertaynement or exceedings be given before Munday on wch and not before the Reading shall beginn, save only wine and bisketts on Sunday morning before hee goes to Church.

Thus the magnificence of the reader's feast gradually waned.

Even in such reveling as this, there was much pageantry: the settings were spectacular, the costumes were rich and impressive, and the measures were stately. These readings show clearly the fondness of the four houses for the histrionic.

B. THE SERGEANTS' FEAST

THE sergeancy at law was an honorary rank equivalent to that of the doctorate.[28] The lord chief justice of the common bench, from time to time, with the concurrence of his associates, selected six or eight of the most learned lawyers in the realm, whose names he submitted to the lord chancellor, who, by power of the king's writ, commanded the presence of the gentlemen so selected to receive the mark of distinction, under great penalty for default.[29] As early as 1521, we have record of four members of the Inner Temple attaining the estate of sergeant, and of the accompanying entertainment with "spices and many comfits (figmenta), with wine of every sort";[30] and, under date of 1567, Stow[31] records a sergeants' feast at Gray's Inn. At this ceremony, the king and queen, the lords and commons, and the mayor and aldermen of London were often guests.

During the morning on which the degrees were to be conferred, wine and cakes were enjoyed by the members of Sergeants' Inn, where these distinguished lawyers resided, and by the gentlemen of the Inn which was to be honored

[28] Fortescue, p. 189.
[29] Dugdale, pp. 111–113.
[30] Inderwick, I, 62–63.
[31] *Annales*, p. 1127.

through granting the sergeancy to its members. After the benchers and barristers had gathered at Sergeants' Inn in processional formation, they proceeded to Westminster, where the sergeants elect and their attendants had gone. After three solemn congees, the sergeants, with each of their fellows initiate, went to the bar of the court, where they made three more congees. The sergeant elect, after being exhorted by the lord chief justice of the king's bench, "declareth upon a real Writ . . . in Law French,"[32] to which the most ancient sergeant made defense; after replication by the sergeant elect, the second ranking sergeant "offereth emparlance thereto;"[33] as this procedure continued until all the sergeants had offered their objections, the legal knowledge of the sergeant elect was severely tested. Then, while the sergeant elect knelt at the feet of the lord chief justice of the king's bench, the oath of office was administered to him, and the lawn coif was placed upon his head and the hood over his shoulders.[34]

The newly elected sergeant was expected to entertain lavishly. It was seldom that any one of the annually created sergeants spent less than £260;[35] each of the fifteen sergeants elected in 1623 paid £600 to the king, in addition to bearing a share of the expense of the feast. Often, apparently following the custom of the Anglo-Saxon host of giving rings to his guests, the sergeants made gifts of valuable rings, instead of money, to the sovereign and to each of his administrative officers. In addition, the sergeants provided cloth for the livery of the servants of the crown and of the Inns of Court. Appendix B gives a typical list of the recipients of rings and cloth. Some further idea of the great expenditure by the newly created sergeants may be gained from the following account:

[32] Dugdale, pp. 137–138.
[33] *Ibid.*
[34] *Ibid.*
[35] Goldsmith, p. 63.

But this you muſt underſtand; that when the day appointed is come; thoſe elect perſons, among other ſolemnities, muſt keep a great dinner, like to the Feaſt of a King's coronation; which shall continue and laſt for the ſpace of ſeven days; and none of thoſe elect perſons shall defray the charges growing to him, about the coſts of this ſolemnity with leſs expences then the ſum of four hundred Marks;[36] ſo that the expences, which eight men ſo elect ſhall then beſtow, will ſurmount to the ſum of three thouſand and two hundred Marks: of which expences one parcel ſhall be this;

Every of them ſhall give Rings of Gold to the value of forty pounds ſterling at the leaſt; and your Chancellor well remembereth, that at what time he received this ſtate and degree, the Rings which he then gave, ſtood him in fifty pounds. For every ſuch Serjeant, at the day of his creation, uſeth to give unto every Prince, Duke, and Archbiſhop being preſent at that ſolemnity; and to the Lord Chancellor and Lord Treaſurer of England, a Ring of the value of xxvis. 8d.

And to every Earl and Biſhop, being likewiſe preſent, and alſo to the Lord Privy Seal; to both the Lords Chief Juſtices, and to the Lord Chief Baron of the King's Exchequer, a Ring of the value of xx s.

And to every Lord Baron of the Parliament; and to every Abbot and notable prelate, and Worſhipful Knight, being then preſent; and alſo to the Maſter of the Rolls, and to every Juſtice, a Ring of the value of a Mark; and likewiſe to every Baron of the Exchequer, to the Chamberlains, and to all the Officers and notable men ſerving in the King's Courts. Rings of a ſmaller price, but agreeable to their Eſtates, to whom they are given.

Inſomuch that there ſhall not be a Clerk, eſpecially in the Court of Common Bench, but he ſhall receive a Ring convenient for his degree: and beſides theſe, they give divers Rings to other to their friends.

They give alſo Liveries of Cloth in one Suit or Colour, in great aboundance; not only to their Houſehold meany, but alſo to their other friends and acquaintance; which during the time of the aforeſaid ſolemnity, ſhall attend and wait upon them. . . .[37]

[36] The amount seems to have varied.

[37] Dugdale, pp. 111–113.

An interesting account of the sergeants' feast of 1532 follows:[38]

In the 23th of King Henry 8th. the *Serjeants Feaſt* was kept in Ely Houſe; the Serjeants then made being in number eleven. . . . Theſe alſo held their Feaſt here for five days;[39] viz. Fryday the 10th. of November, Saturday, Sunday, Monday, and Tueſday. . . . On Monday, which was their principall day King Henry and Queen Catherine dined there (but in two Chambers) and the forein Embaſſdors in a third Chamber.

In the Hall, at the high Table sate Sir Nicholas Lambard Maior of London; the Judges; the Barons of the Exchequer, with certain Aldermen of the City.

At the board on the South ſide sate the Maſter of the Rolls, the Maſters of the Chancery, and Worſhipfull Citizens: On the North ſide of the Hall certain Aldermen began the Board; and then followed Merchants of the City. In the Cloyſtry, Chapell and Gallery, Knights, Eſquires, and Gentlemen were placed.

In the Halls, the Crafts of London: The Serjeants at Law, and their Wives, kept in their own Chambers.

It were tedious to ſet down the preparation of Fiſh, Fleſh, and other Victualls ſpent in this Feaſt, and would ſeem almoſt incredible; and (as to me it ſeemeth) wanted little of a Feaſt at a Coronation: Neverthelеſſ a little I will touch, for declaration of the change of prices.

There were brought to the ſlaughter-Houſe twenty four great Beefes at	01*l* 06*s* 08*d*	the piece.
From the Shambles one Carcaſs of an Oxe at	01–04–00	
One hundred fat Muttons at	00–02–10	a piece.
Fifty one great Veales at	00–04–08	a piece.
Thirty four Porkes	00–03–03	a piece.
Ninety one Piggs	00–00–06	a piece.

[38] *Ibid.*, pp. 127–128. Herbert, pp. 374–375, in describing this feast, follows Dugdale closely.

[39] The length of time of this feast by the sergeants seems to have covered from five to seven days.

Capon of Greece, of one Poulter (for they had 3.) ten dozen at	00–01–08	the piece.
Capons of Kent nine dozen and ſix, at	00–01–00	a piece.
Cocks of groſe ſeaven dozen and nine, at	00–00–08	a piece.
Cocks courſe xiiii dozen at 8*d.* and three pence a piece.		
Pullets the beſt	00–00–02	ob.
Other pullets	00–00–02	
Pidgeons 37 dozens, at	00–00–10	the dozen.
Swans xiiii. dozen.		
Larkes 340 dozen, at 5*d* the dozen.		

Edward Nevill was Seneſcall or Steward, Thomas Ratcliffe Controller, Thomas Wilden Clerke of the Kitchen.[40]

[40] While this list, in itself, is imposing, yet when the great number served and the length of the feast (5 days), are considered, the provisions seem to have been no more than adequate. It should be remembered, too, that England, during the sixteenth century, was largely carnivorous. This list does not compare with the amount of provisions for a single passage of a large trans-Atlantic liner, for example, the length of time and number of guests being approximately the same as at the sergeants' feast. It is believed that the abundance of food at many English feasts of this period has been overestimated.

CHAPTER IV

Political Revels

THE comity subsisting between the crown and the Inns of Court was intensified by acts of friendship and gallantry by the gentlemen of the Inns to celebrate or commemorate any event of importance in the lives of the royal family.

In 1501, members of the Middle Temple attended, and perhaps participated in, the jousts and tourneys in honor of the marriage of Katherine of Aragon and Prince Arthur; and, in 1509, a levy was imposed upon members of the Inner Temple for "lez standyngges" at "le justes" in celebration of the coronation of Henry and Katherine, at which time "out of the mouthes of certain beastes or gargels did runne red, white, and claret wine."[1] With the birth of a child to Katherine, another levy was imposed upon the gentlemen of the Temple; at this time, "wyne was set for suche as woulde take thereof in certayne streates in London."[2] A few days later, there was tilting, in which the dramatic element was pronounced, for the king, as the "Knight *Cure Loial*," held the field, aided by "the Earl of Devonshire as *Bon Voloire*, Sir Thomas Knevet as *Bon Espoir*, and Sir Edward Neville as *Valiaunt Desire*."[3] But, much before this, in 7 Edward IV (1468), the gentlemen of the four Inns provided armed guard for the jousts between "Wydeville lord Scales and the bastard son of the duke of Burgundy."[4] The gentlemen of Lincoln's Inn, in a body, attended the coronation day festivities of 1532, after which there was feasting

[1] Williamson, p. 138, and Hall, pp. 510–511.

[2] Williamson, p. 138, and Hall, pp. 516, *et seq.*

[3] *Ibid.*

[4] Herbert, p. 313.

("*in convivio*") at "le Kynges Hed" by the gentlemen of the four Inns.[5] The gentlemen of Lincoln's also observed the coronation of King Henry VIII by providing scaffolds at Westminster to "see the joustings and tiltings," after which they cheered themselves with a hogshead of claret wine.[6]

One of the most popular of public rejoicings was the lighting of bonfires, survivals of the sun charms used at medieval agricultural feasts, in which ritual and revelry were blended. The bonfire was used, during the sixteenth and seventeenth centuries, to celebrate the return of the sovereign from a journey, much as today we honor the return of the chief magistrate with a salute of guns. Bonfires were built when the queen returned in 1625,[7] when Charles I returned from the North, when his queen completed her journey from Portugal, when James II returned from Rochester, and when William and Mary came as sovereigns of England.[8] Bonfires were also lighted to celebrate the birth of a son to Charles I, and, in 1631, to observe the birth of a daughter[9] to the same sovereign, whose coronation day was kept similarly.[10] Moreover, they were kindled on political holidays, such as Guy Fawkes's Day, November 5. They also formed a part of the observance of church holidays.[11] These bonfires were probably lighted in Fleet Street near the Temple gate.

[5] Black Book, I, 253–256 (1532–33).

[6] Herbert, p. 313.

[7] Inderwick, II, 152.

[8] Inner Temple General Account Book 1687–88.

[9] Inderwick, II, 201.

[10] *Ibid.*

[11] The fire rite at the Inns will be discussed in connection with the Christmas revels.

CHAPTER V

Ecclesiastical Revels

A. THE FEASTS OF ALL SAINTS AND THE PURIFICATION

IN 1508–9, the gentlemen of Lincoln's Inn were entertained on Purification day by minstrels, at a cost of forty shillings;[1] and in 1581, on the same day, these gentlemen acted as hosts to their colleagues of the Middle Temple.[2] The coöperation of the various houses was secured in no better way than through such interhostel banqueting.

In 1606–7, on Candlemas day, the gentlemen of the Inner Temple were entertained with a play, which cost five pounds, and on the evening preceding, lighted torches, which cost two shillings, formed part of the pageant-like display. During the same year, on All-Hallows day, musicians were paid twenty shillings.[3] Another play was presented before the same gentlemen on Candlemas day in 1608–9; and during the Michaelmas term three revels were held at a cost of three pounds.[4] During the following year, these gentlemen were entertained with plays on both All-Hallows day and Candlemas day.[5] In 1612, a "consort" of music was given on All-Hallows at a cost of fifty shillings, and "antics or puppits" diverted the students, at a cost of forty shillings. On Candlemas day of the same year, six pounds was paid for a play, an increase of one pound over the usual price. The cost of sack seems to have increased proportionately.[6] In 1670, at

[1] Black Book, I, 154.
[2] Bellot, p. 313.
[3] Inderwick, II, 31.
[4] *Ibid.*, pp. 44–45.
[5] *Ibid.*, p. 53.
[6] *Ibid.*, p. 70.

the feast of the Purification at Gray's Inn, "his Majesty was present, accompanied by most of the Court in masquerade."[7]

B. CHRISTMAS CELEBRATION

CHRISTMAS frolics usually continued for four weeks, from the Monday preceding St. Thomas' day (December 21) to the Saturday in the week following Epiphany (January 6), and were called the week of St. Thomas, the week of the Nativity, the week of the Epiphany, and the week after the Epiphany, or, more simply, the first, second, third, and fourth weeks of Christmas.[8]

For entertainment during these weeks, a mock prince or king was crowned, and each of the Inns was transformed into a court. This officer was called the Prince of Purpoole[9] at Gray's Inn, the Prince de la Grange at Lincoln's Inn, Prince of Sophie at the Inner Temple, and Prince d'Amour at the Middle Temple. Sometimes the prince existed independently of the king; at other times, they were coexistent. At Lincoln's Inn, the Christmas king was called the King of Cocknies,[10] whose foil during the early sixteenth century was Jack Straw, an anti-king.[11] The Christmas prince at the Inns, therefore, burlesquing the sovereign, was the civil analogue of the boy bishop, who burlesqued the ecclesiastical officer whose name he took. It has been maintained that the Christmas prince had his origin in the boy bishop.[12] It is thought, however, that

[7] Fletcher, II, 14. [8] Inderwick, II, 87.

[9] Named for the parish in which Gray's lies.

[10] From cockered child, or mother's darling. The King of Cocknies was specially enjoined to "medyll neither in the buttry, nor in the stuard of Christmass his office upon pain of xls. for every such medling" (Black Book, I, 189–190).

[11] "Item that Jack Strawe and all his adherentes be from hensforth uttrely banyshed and no more to be vsed in Lincolles Inne, uppon peyne to forfeyt for euery tyme fyue poundes" (February 9, 1519, Black Book, I, 189–190).

[12] Dawson, pp. 155–156, quoting account of the 1607 Christmas, published in 1816 by Robert Tripbook, 23 Old Bond Street, London.

such a position is not entirely tenable, for burlesquing officers at the Inns seem to be of quite as ancient standing as the boy bishop. The custom of electing both officers was probably the survival of the practice of medieval people in choosing a sovereign to reign over them during their agricultural mummings.[13] The master of the revels[14] continued to exercise his office as director. Of less importance were the marshal (*Marescallus*),[15] the butler (*Pincerna*), the constable marshal, the server, and the cupbearer. At the Inner Temple, a clerk of the kitchen (*Clericus Coquinae*), a master of the game,[16] and a constable of the tower (*Constabularius Turris* or *ad Turrim*), were appointed in addition to the regular officers. The imitation of the officers of court and state seems to have been not only for the amusement derived from burlesquing them, but quite as much for the training of the gentlemen of the Inns for future service as officers of court and state:

> Hit is agreed and ordeyned that he that shalbe chosen hereafter to be Kyng ouer Cristmas Day shall occupy then the seid rowme[17] if he be present, . . . for lernyng of yong Gentilmen to do seruice, . . . [18] [and] which officers for the most part are such as are exercised in the King's highness house and other noblemen and this is done onely to the intent that they should in time to come know how to use themselves.[19]

On January 8, 1635, the Rev. Mr. G. Garrard wrote to the Earl of Strafford a letter descriptive of the Christmas prince:

> The Middle Temple House have set up a prince, who carries himself in great state: . . . He hath all his great officers attending him, lord keeper, lord treasurer, eight white staves at the least, cap-

[13] Welsford, p. 3.

[14] Usually an utter barrister.

[15] Usually a bencher.

[16] A similar officer was elected at the agricultural mummings.

[17] Room, office, or post.

[18] Black Book, I, 189–190.

[19] Williamson, p. 109; Waterhouse, p. 546.

tain of his pensioners, captain of his guard, two chaplains, who on Sunday last preached before him, and in the pulpit made three low legs to his excellency before they began, which is much laughed at. My lord chamberlain lent him two fair cloths of state, one hung up in the hall under which he dines, the other in his privy chamber; he is served on the knee, and all that come to see him kiss his hand on their knee. My lord of Salisbury hath sent him pole-axes for his pensioners. He sent to my lord of Holland, his justice in Eyre, for venison, which he willingly sends him; to the lord mayor and sheriffs of London for wine, all obey. Twelfth-day was a great day, going to the chapel many petitions were delivered him, which he gave to his masters of the requests. He hath a favourite, whom with some others, gentlemen of great quality, he knighted at his return from church, and dined in great state; at the going out of the chambers into the garden, when he drank the King's health, the glass being at his mouth he let it fall, which much defaced his purple satten suit, for so he was clothed that day, having a cloak of the same down to his foot, for he mourns for his father who lately died. It cost this prince £2,000 out of his own purse. I hear of no other design, but that all this is done to make them fit to give the prince elector a royal entertainment with masks, dancings, and some other exercises of wit, in orations or arraignments, that day that they invite him.[20]

As the weather at Christmas usually did not permit engaging in outdoor sports, such as tennis,[21] or barriers,[22] or bowling,[23] indoor diversions, particularly dicing, were popular. Gambling during the holidays was, for a long while, permitted to the students. On St. Thomas' eve, an order was

[20] Quoted by Dawson, pp. 155–156. This prince was knighted by the King (Bellot, p. 182), as was Mr. Rich, master of the revels at Lincoln's Inn during 1670–71 (Black Book, III, 451).

[21] James Hooker and Anne Tyler were sued by Lincoln's Inn for building on the ground intended for a "rackett courte" (Black Book, II, 414).

[22] A tilt-yard sport (Fletcher, Introduction, I, xxxix).

[23] At Gray's, bowling was prohibited during term time (*ibid.*, I, 320), and laundresses were forbidden to dry clothing on the "bouleing Greene" (*ibid.*, I, 306).

granted for the setting up of tables for play,[24] and, at another time, Gwillim was commanded to "treat with the box keepers concerning the furnishing of their own tables with dice.[25] When the floor of the Middle Temple hall was removed about two hundred years ago, nearly a hundred pairs of yellowed dice were found.[26] Under the heading "necessaries" in the daily records of the Inner Temple appear the following typical items: "dice and cards, 7li. 13s.; casting boxes, 23*s.* 4*d.*,"[27] and "4 dozen casting boxes, 8s.; dice 1 li. 14s."[28]

During the Christmas season, the floor of the hall of each of the Inns was strewn with sawdust and rushes;[29] candles and torches were lighted in profusion;[30] silverware, including finger bowls, ewers, and rosewater basins, adorned the cupboard; and the tables were covered with the best "sleazey diaper." Quantities of food were served on platters, and of drink in green earthenware or silver cups. The records of the Inner Temple are eloquent regarding the supplies for entertainment during these four weeks. The following items of expenditure are more or less representative:

Milk for rice pottage, eggs for moonshine, "chesemittes," "scerrettes,"[31] eggs for "Florantynes," "Oryngadoe," brawn,[32] suet for minced pies, 12 lb., anchovies, ox eyes,[33] 39 marrow-bones, 19 mallards, 18 shoulders of mutton, 20 dozen larks,[34] a gallon of burnt claret, and a gallon of buttered ale and sack,[35] ale for "sowsinge drincke," hippocras, blackbirds, 9 doz.,[36] chicks for settell soppes, 19, butter for paste and chickens for "sorrell sopps,"[37] 24 udders and

[24] Inderwick, III, 54.
[25] *Ibid.*, p. 130.
[26] *The Hall*, published by Abram.
[27] Inderwick, II, 159.
[28] *Ibid.*, III, 184.
[29] *Ibid.*, II, 87.
[30] "Playford's bill for lights on Christmas night, 1 li. 14s. 6d." (*Ibid.*, III, 184).
[31] *Ibid.*, II, 105.
[32] *Ibid.*, p. 93.
[33] *Ibid.*, p. 135.
[34] *Ibid.*, p. 87.
[35] *Ibid.*, p. 185.
[36] *Ibid.*, p. 122.
[37] *Ibid.*, p. 111.

tongues, the vintner's bill of the King's Head, 12s. 11d.,[38] rabbit suckers, 26 "Jerusalem hartichockes,"[39] and smelts to fry.[40]

At Christmas, 1677, an account was taken of the beer remaining at the Inner Temple, at which time it was found that ninety barrels of small beer and six barrels of strong beer were on hand.[41] That the olfactory sense might not be offended, Black Jack was paid four shillings sixpence for "candle and perfume."[42] Sufficient music, also, was provided: "lowd music, 20 s,[43] the harper, two nights, 10s,[44] to the trumpetters, 11s,[45] the music 10 li,[46] music 27 li. 1s. 8d., the drum and fife, 10s,"[47] etc. The music room was usually specially decorated for the Christmas holidays: "Green say for the music room hangings, 5s,"[48] and "Mending the cloth for the music room, 18 d."[49] Various items appear covering tobacco, in addition to that for "scerrettes," which may possibly mean cigarettes: "Tobacco, 2s.,"[50] and "more smoke, 1s."[51] Expenditures for paraphernalia for officers assisting the Christmas king are very common: "For hire of 'holbeards,[52] coats, and vesserdes,'[53, 54] the halbert mending,[55] a plume of white feathers, and another of black, for the controller, 8 li.,[56] 'trunches[57] and whyt stafes,'[58] and ribbon for their helmets."[59] That arms were fired is evident from the following: "Dinner for the gunners, 6s," and "For the ordnance, twice, 10 li."[60] The accounts indicate, also, the nature of professional entertainment: "For the 'tumlers,' 15s,"[61] and "For

38 Inderwick, II, p. 192.
39 *Ibid.*, p. 128.
40 *Ibid.*, p. 111.
41 *Ibid.*, III, 129.
42 *Ibid.*, p. 184.
43 *Ibid.*, II, 105.
44 *Ibid.*, III, 184.
45 *Ibid.*, II, 116.
46 *Ibid.*, p. 87.
47 *Ibid.*, p. 93.
48 *Ibid.*, p. 128.
49 *Ibid.*, p. 93.
50 *Ibid.*, p. 93.
51 *Ibid.*
52 *Ibid.*, p. 122; halberds.
53 *Ibid.*
54 Vizards.
55 Inderwick, II, 111, 116.
56 *Ibid.*, III, 184.
57 *Ibid.*, II, 93; truncheons.
58 *Ibid.*, p. 93.
59 *Ibid.*
60 *Ibid.*
61 *Ibid.*, p. 116.

sweetmeats for Madam Gwinn, 1 li."[62] During the celebrations, the poor were always comforted: "To the poor in the kitchen, 5s.,"[63] but special searches were made for thieves, who were committed to jail: "The jailors' fees, 6s. 8d.; his men, 2s.; to the watch, 2s.; the jury, 2s."[64] In 1617, William was reimbursed for his hat, which was probably lost in the excitement,[65] and the surgeon was paid four shillings "for healing the poor man that was cut."[66]

On Christmas eve, the revels officers occupied the highest places at the tables, to which the benchers proceeded, attended by the butlers with lighted torches. An occasional address was then delivered by the senior bencher, after which carols were sung before the hearth, about which the musicians were grouped. After dinner was served, dancing and singing were enjoyed, which continued until supper. One of the popular songs immediately following the Restoration was the following:

MERRY BOYS OF CHRISTMAS,
OR
THE MILK-MAID'S NEW YEAR'S GIFT

When Lads and Lasses take delight,
together for to be;
They pass away the Winter night,
and live most merrily.

To the tune of, *Hey boys up go we.*

Come, come my roaring ranting boys
lets never be cast down,
We'll never mind the female toys,
but Loyal be to th' Crown:

[62] Nell Gwynn, who played at the Inner Temple on January 12, 1682; *ibid.*, III, 184.

[63] E.g., *ibid.*, II, 159.

[64] *Ibid.*, p. 93.

[65] *Ibid.*, p. 105.

[66] *Ibid.*, p. 184.

We'll never break our hearts with care,
nor be cast down with fear,
Our bellys then let us prepare
to drink some Christmas Beer.

Then here's a health to Charles our King,
throughout the world admir'd,
Let us his great applauses sing,
that we so much desir'd,
And wisht amongst us for to reign,
when Oliver rul'd here.
But since he's home return'd again,
come fill some Christmas Beer.

These holidays we'll briskly drink,
all mirth we will devise,
No Treason we will speak or think,
then bring us brave minc'd pies:
Roast Beef and brave Plum-porridge,
our Loyal hearts to chear,
Then prithee make no more ado,
but bring us Christmas Beer.[67]

When coals were brought to the hearth, the gentlemen danced three times about the fire. This was a survival from more primitive times: three is still a magic number; the fire represented the sun, both in shape and in attribute.[68] The sun was, of course, apotheosized by undeveloped agricultural races as the source of heat and light, the benignant ripener of grains. In the dark ages, the building of a fire, as a mark of homage to the sun, always formed a part of the ceremony of the agricultural feast.[69] At each of the Inns, about this glowing fire in the center of the great hall, which

[67] Dawson, p. 215; taken from ballad in library of the British Museum.

[68] The figure of the sun has long been used as emblematic of the law and of the legal profession; it was formerly used on garments, and particularly on the collars, of justices of rank.

[69] Chambers, *Med.*, I, 125; Welsford, p. 3.

was embowered with holly and bay, the young gentlemen danced about the fire in procession, singing "Round about Our Coal Fire." This song has been lost,[70] but others, like the following,[71] which were probably sung, have descended to us:

I

O You merry, merry Souls,
Christmas is a comming,
We shall have flowing Bowls,
Dancing, piping, drumming.

II

Delicate Minced Pies,
To feast every Virgin,
Capon and goose likewise,
Brawn and a Dish of Sturgeon.

III

Then for your Christmas Box.
Sweet Plumb Cakes and Money,
Delicate Holland Smocks,
Kisses sweet as Honey.

IV

Hey for the Christmas Ball,
Where we shall be jolly,
Jigging short and tall,
Kate, Dick, Ralph, and Molly.

V

Then to the Hop we'll go,
Where we'll jig and caper,
Maidens all-a-row,
Will shall pay the Scraper.

[70] The booklet *Round about Our Coal Fire* portrays well the usual Christmas celebration.

[71] *Round about Our Coal Fire*, prologue.

VI

Hodge shall dance with Prue,
Keeping Time with Kisses
We'll have a jovial Crew,
Of sweet smirking Misses.

On Christmas day, the first course, a boar's head, was brought into the hall on an immense salver by the butlers, accompanied by the musicians, who played all the while. At the universities, where this custom existed also, and probably at the Inns, the following song[72] was sung by the gentlemen:

Caput afri differo
Reddens laudes domino.

The bore's heed in hand bring I,
With garlans gay and rosemary,
I pray you all synge merely
Qui estis in convivio.

The bore's heed, I vnderstande,
Is the chefe seruyce in this lande;
Loke, where euer it be fande,
Seruite cum cantico.

Be gladde lordes, bothe more and lasse,
For this hath ordeyned our stewarde,
To chere you all this Christmasse,
The bores heed with mustarde.

This curious custom, which perseveres today in holiday displays in restaurants, where the boar's head is found with an apple or a lemon in its mouth, as a mark of abundance or fertility, has its origin in pagan worship, closely connected with adoration of the sun. Fro, or Freyr, the Germanic and Norse god of light, benevolence, and fertility, rode, as did his sister Freyja, on a boar with golden bristles, symbolic of

[72] From Sandys, p. 231.

Entertainment of Charles II at One of the Inns

Bringing in the Boar's Head

the beaming rays of the sun. Thus, the snout of the boar's head which was served at feasts was often gilded, and sometimes a crown of gold was placed upon the head of this "sovereign beast." Just as the cow has become a sacred symbol of fertility in India, so the boar in Germanic countries became a somewhat sacred emblem; but, unlike the Indians, who protect the cow by taboo, the Germanic peoples began to feed on the boar, and it became indispensable at all gatherings at which the blessing of Fro was adjured.[73] Gradually brawn or the entire head of the boar became the principal food at feasts of any nature.[74]

Medieval mummers, during the seasons of the year when their food supply was imperiled by caprices of nature, often gathered to hunt in the woods.[75] The Christmas hunt at the Inns of Court has never been entirely understood, but it is thought that it, too, is a survival of the tradition of the dark ages. It may be the protraction of a form of worship of Diana. The records of Lincoln's Inn show that, in 1590, the hunt at Kentish Town was prohibited.[76] Whether an actual expedition was made to Kentish Town and whether a genuine hunt was held there may not be ascertained, but, as officers of the hunt (called the master or keeper of the game and the ranger), were elected annually, we may perhaps assume that a mimic hunt, at least, was engaged in.[77] We know that, on St. Stephen's day, the officers of the hunt, having entered the hall clad in green satin or velvet, en-

[73] Karl Blind, II, *Saga-Book of the Viking Club*.

[74] Extracts from Inner Temple accounts: "the Society shall have for Christmas one boar," "the company . . . shall have . . . paid to them . . . 30s. for a boar, minstrels, and a load of coals," and "one 'le bore,' and . . . minstrels at Christmas, 30s., and a cartload of coals" (Inderwick, I, 75, 139, and 89, respectively).

[75] Welsford, p. 3.

[76] "It ys ordered . . . that the repair vsuallye at a certayne daye of the year to Kentishe Towne . . . shalbe taken awaye and noe more vsed" (Black Book, II, 16).

[77] *Ibid.*, II, 16 n.

circled the fire, blowing their horns three times. A cat and a fox, brought in by a huntsman, were then, within the hall, set upon by perhaps twenty hounds, which, aided by the huntsmen, drove the cat and the fox into the fire, where they were burned to death.[78] This traditional practice, so decried as unbecoming enlightened young gentlemen, was a remnant of ancient custom which combined various animal superstitions with the fire rite or heat charm. Pagan worshipers of heat thought that contact with fire would render them, and their animals, free from disease and would make them fertile.[79] Hence, the driving of cattle through smoke or smoldering ashes became a part of the seasonal feast. The cat and the fox, like the squirrel and the owl, were often considered to be tree spirits, and, therefore, symbolic of vegetation in general or of corn.[80] Thus, as these animals were revered, their destruction was interdicted. During feasts of husbandry, however, they were not protected by taboo; at this time, they were driven into the fire as an appeal for preservation against pestilence.[81]

The best extant description of any of these Christmas celebrations is that of Gerard Legh (Leigh),[82] who depicts with great particularity the grand Christmas at the Inner Temple of 1561–62. This quaint but enlightening description follows:[83]

After I had travailed through the East parts of the unknown world, to understand of deedes of armes, and so arriving in the fair river of Thames, I landed within half a league from the City of London, which was (as I conjecture) in December last; and drawing neer the City, suddenly heard the shot of double canons, in so a great a number, and so terrible, that it darkened the

[78] Dawson, p. 125. [79] Chambers, *Med.*, I, 125.

[80] N. W. Thomas, "Animal Superstitions and Totemism," *Folk-Lore*, II, 257.

[81] Welsford, p. 23; Nichols, *Elizabeth*, I, 131–141.

[82] *Accedens of Armory*, pp. 119, *et seq.;* also described by Dugdale.

[83] Legh has been collated with Nichols (*Progresses of Elizabeth*, pp. 131, *et seq.* of Vol. I), from whom quotation is actually taken.

whole ayr; wherewith, although I was in my native country, yet stood I amazed, not knowing what it meant. Thus, as I abode in despair, either to return or continue my former purpose, I chanced to see coming towards me an honest citizen, clothed in a long garment, keeping the highway, seeming to walk for his recreation, which prognosticated rather peace than perill; of whom I demanded the cause of this great shot; who friendly answered, "It is," quoth he, "a warning shot to the Constable Marshall of the Inner Temple, to prepare to dinner."

"Why," said I, "what, is he of that estate, that seeketh no other means to warn his officers than with so terrible shot in so peaceable a country?" "Marry," saith he, "he uttereth himself the better to be that Officer whose name he beareth."

I then demanded, "what province did he govern, that needed such an officer?" He answered me, "The province was not great in quantity, but antient in true nobility. A place," said he, "privileged by the most excellent Princess the High Governor of the whole Island, wherein are store of Gentlemen of the whole Realm, that repair thither to learn to rule and obey by Law, to yield their fleece to their Prince and Commonweal; as also to use all other exercises of body and mind whereunto nature most aptly serveth to adorn, by speaking, countenance, gesture, and use of apparel, the person of a Gentleman; whereby amity is obtained, and continued, that Gentlemen of all countries, in their young years, nourished together in one place, with such comely order, and daily conference, are knit by continual acquaintance in such unity of mindes and manners as lightly never after is severed, than which is nothing more profitable to the Commonweale."

And after he had told me thus much of honour of the place, I commended in mine own conceit the policy of the Governour, which seemed to utter in itself the foundation of a good Commonweal; for that, the best of their people from tender years trained up in precepts of justice, it could not choose but yield forth a profitable People to a wise Commonweal; wherefore I determined with myself to make proof of what I heard by report.

The next day I thought for my pastime to walk to this Temple, and entring in at the gates, I found the building nothing costly; but many comely Gentlemen of face and person, and thereto very courteous, saw I to pass to and fro, so as it seemed a Prince's port to be at hand: and passing forward, entred into a Church of antient building, wherein were many monuments of noble personages armed in knightly habit, with their cotes depainted in ancient shields, whereat I took pleasure to behold. Thus gazing as one bereft with the rare sight, there came unto me an Hereaught, by name Palaphilos, a King of Armes, who curteously saluted me, saying, "For that I was a stranger, and seeming by my demeanour a lover of honour, I was his guest of right:" whose curtesy (as reason was) I obeyed; answering, "I was at his commandment."

"Then," said he, "Ye shall go to mine own lodging here within the Palace, where we will have such cheer as the time and country will yield us:" where, I assure you, I was so entertained, as no where I met with better cheer or company, &c.

—Thus talking, we entred the Prince his Hall, where anon we heard the noise of drum and fyfe. "What meaneth this drum?" said I. Quoth he, "This is to warn Gentlemen of the Household to repair to the dresser; wherefore come on with me, and ye shall stand where ye may best see the Hall served": and so from thence brought me into a long gallery, that stretched itself along the Hall neer the Prince's table, where I saw the Prince set: a man of tall personage, a manly countenance, somewhat brown of visage, strongly featured, and thereto comely proportioned in all lineaments of body. At the nether end of the same table were placed the Embassadors of sundry Princes. Before him stood the carver, sewer, and cup-bearer, with great number of gentlemen-wayters attending his person; the ushers making place to strangers of sundry regions that came to behold the honour of this mighty Captain. After the placing of these honourable guests, the Lord Steward, Treasurer, and Keeper of Pallas Seal, with divers honourable personages of that Nobility, were placed at a side-table neer adjoining the Prince on the right hand: and at another table, on the left side, were placed the Treasurer of the Household, Secretary, the Prince his Serjeant at the Law, four Masters of the Revels, the King of Arms, the Dean of the Chappel, and divers Gentlemen Pensioners to furnish the same.[84]

[84] See Appendix C for complete list of officers, among them being Lord Robert Dudley (later Earl of Leicester), Roger Manwood (later Lord Chief

At another table, on the other side, were set the Master of the Game, and his Chief Ranger, Masters of Household, Clerks of the Green Cloth and Check, with divers other strangers to furnish the same.

On the other side against them, began the table, the Lieutenant of the Tower, accompanied with divers Captains of foot-bands and shot. At the nether end of the Hall began the table, the High Butler, the Panter, Clerks of the Kitchin, Master Cook of the Privy Kitchin, furnished throughout with the souldiers and guard of the Prince: all which, with number of inferior officers placed and served in the Hall, besides the great resort of strangers, I spare to write.

The prince so served with tender meats, sweet fruits, and dainty delicates confectioned with curious cookery, as it seemed wonder a world to observe the provision: and at every course the trumpetters blew the couragious blast of deadly war, with noise of drum and fyfe, with the sweet harmony of violins, sackbutts, recorders, and cornetts, with other instruments of musick, as it seemed Apollo's harp had tuned their stroke.

Thus the Hall was served after the most ancient order of the Island; in commendation whereof I say I have also seen the service of great Princes, in solemn seasons and times of triumph, yet the order hereof was not inferior to any.

But to proceed, this Herehaught Palaphilos, even before the second course came in, standing at the high table, said in this manner: "The mighty Palaphilos, Prince of Sophie, High Constable Marshall of the Knights Templars, Patron of the Honorable Order of Pegasus:" and therewith cryeth, "A largess." The Prince, praysing the Herehaught, bountifully rewarded him with a chain to the value of an hundred talents.

I assure you, I languish for want of cunning, ripely to utter that I saw so orderly handled appertaining to service; wherefore I cease, and return to my purpose.

The supper ended, and tables taken up, the High Constable rose, and a while stood under the place of honour, where his atchievement

Baron), and Christopher Hatton (later Lord Chancellor of England). At this feast, twenty-four gentlemen of the Inn were made knights of the Order of Pegasus.

was beautifully embroidered, and devised of sundry matters, with the Ambassadors of foreign nations, as he thought good, till Palaphilos, King of Armes, came in, his Herehaught Marshal, and Pursuivant before him; and after followed his messenger and Caligate Knight; who putting off his coronal, made his humble obeysance to the Prince, by whom he was commanded to draw neer, and understand his pleasure; saying to him, in few words, to this effect: "Palaphilos, seeing it hath pleased the high Pallas, to think me to demerit the office of this place; and thereto this night past vouchsafed to descend from heavens to increase my further honour, by creating me Knight of her Order of Pegasus; as also commanded me to join in the same Society such valiant Gentlemen throughout her province, whose living honour hath best deserved the same, the choice whereof most aptly belongeth to your skill, being the watchman of their doings, and register of their deserts; I will ye choose as well throughout our whole armyes, as elsewhere, of such special gentlemen, as the gods hath appointed, the number of twenty-four, and the names of them present us: commanding also those chosen persons to appear in our presence in knightly habit, that with conveniency we may proceed in our purpose." This done, Palaphilos obeying his Prince's commandment, with twenty-four valiant Knights, all apparelled in long white vestures, with each man a scarf of Pallas colours, and them presented, with their names, to the Prince; who allowed well his choise, and commanded him to do his office. Who, after his duty to the Prince, bowed towards these worthy personages, standing every man in his antienty, as he had born armes in the field, and began to shew his Prince's pleasure; with the honour of the Order.

Precepts governing the conduct of each of the officers were definitely established. For instance, on St. Stephen's day, the constable marshal, preceded by drummers, mounted a scaffold borne by four men, and encircled the hearth three times, crying "A Lord, a lord," after which he summoned his court in the following, or similar, burlesque terms:

Sir Francis Flatterer, of Fowleshurst, in the county of Buckingham.
Sir Randle Rakabite, of Rascall-hall, in the county of Rake-hell.

Sir Morgan Mumchance, of Much Monkery, in the county of Mad Mopery.[85]

Sir Bartholomew Baldbreech, of Buttocks-bury, in the county of Brekeneck.[86]

Machyn's[87] description of this celebration follows:

> The xxvij day of Desember cam ryding thrugh London a lord of mysrull, in clene complett harnes, gylt, with a hondred grett horse and gentyll-men rydyng gorgyously with chenes of gold, and there horses godly trapytt, unto the Tempull, for ther was grett cher all Cryustynmas tyll [blank], and grett revels as ever was for the gentyllmen of the Tempull evere day, for mony of the conselle was there [blank] of myssrule [blank] playhyng and syngyng unto the [court with my?] lord, ther was grett chere at the [blank] gorgyously apparrell[ed] with grett cheynes.

One of the most ostentatious of the Christmas celebrations was that held at Gray's Inn in 1594–95. An entire record of this festivity is to be found in *Gesta Grayorum*,[88] the title-page of which follows:

Gefta Grayorum:

OR, THE

HISTORY

Of the High and mighty PRINCE,

HENRY

Prince of Purpoole, Arch-Duke of Stapulia and Bernardia, Duke of High and Nether Holborn, Marquis of St. Giles and Tottenham, Count Palatine of Bloomsbury and Clerkenwell, Great Lord of the Cantons of Iflington, Kentifh-Town, Paddington and Knights-bridge,

[85] Sometimes "Popery," which destroys the alliteration.

[86] Nichols, *Elizabeth*, I, 140; Dugdale, pp. 150–157; Herbert, pp. 256, *et seq.*

[87] *Diary*, pp. 273–274, year 1561.

[88] Included in Nichols' *Elizabeth*, III, 262, and in Appendix to Brown's *Law Sports at Gray's Inn*; reprinted by Malone and others. Where and when Canning obtained the manuscript are not known.

Knight of the moſt Heroical Order of the
Helmet, and Sovereign of the Same:
Who Reigned and Died, A. D. 1594.

TOGETHER WITH

A Maſque,[89] as it was preſented (by His Highneſs's Command) for the Entertainment of Q. ELIZABETH; who, with the Nobles of both Courts, was preſent thereat.

LONDON, Printed for W. Canning, at his Shop in the Temple-Cloyſters, MDCLXXXVIII.
Price one Shilling.

After many consultations, the gentlemen of Gray's chose Henry Holmes (Hulme or Helme), of Norfolk, to be Prince of Purpoole, to whom they gave jurisdiction over the parish in which Gray's is situated[90] and over neighboring parishes to which resort was often had during the celebration.[91] Moreover, the prince was given authority over the two Inns of Chancery, Staple Inn and Barnard's Inn.[92] A complete administrative staff, including a privy council, was appointed to advise the prince.[93]

Communications were directed to gentlemen within the bailiwick of the prince but nonresident in the house, enjoining them not only to attend the Christmas festivity but to make a contribution to defray the expense thereof, upon pain of being "proclaimed in our publick assemblies, to their great discredit." Among the donors was Sir William Cecil, Lord Treasurer of England, who sent ten pounds and an embroidered purse.

The gentlemen of Gray's then sent the following letter

[89] *The Masque of Proteus,* which will be considered later.
[90] Portpool.
[91] Hunting expedition was made to Kentish Town on St. Stephen's day.
[92] "Arch Duke of STAPULIA and BERNARDIA."
[93] Appendix D gives a complete list of officers of state.

to their ancient allies, the gentlemen of the Inner Temple, requesting ambassadorial representation:

To the most Honourable and Prudent, the Governors,
Assistants, and Society
of the *Inner Temple.*

Most Grave and Noble,

We have, upon good consideration, made choice of a Prince, to be predominant in our State of *Purpoole,* for some important causes that require an head, or leader: and as we have ever had great cause, by the warrant of experience, to assure ourselves of your unfeigned love and amity, so we are, upon this occasion, and in the name of our Prince elect, to pray you, that it may continue; and in demonstration thereof, that you will be pleased to assist us with your counsel, in the person of an Ambassador, that may be resident here amongst us, and be a minister of correspondence between us, and to advise of such affairs, as the effects whereof, we hope, shall sort to the benefit of both our estates. And so, being ready to requite you with all good offices, we leave you to the protection of the Almighty.

Your most loving friend and ally,

GRAY'S-INN.

Dated at our Court of Graya, this 14th of December, 1594.[94]

The gentlemen of the Inner Temple accepted this invitation quite as flatulently as it was tendered.

On December 20, 1594, the prince, accompanied by a stately train, promenaded to the hall, where he was enthroned; at this time his sovereignty was proclaimed by the King at Arms. After this, the prince's champion, riding, in complete armor, about the fire, gaged his gauntlet in protection of the prince. The prince's arms were then blazoned.

After the attorney had extolled the excellences of the prince and had exhorted the citizenry to reverence and obedience, the prince vouchsafed that he would be "a gracious and loving Prince to so well deserving subjects."

The solicitor then gave an account of the "puissant poten-

[94] Nichols, *Elizabeth,* III, 264.

tates" who were "feodaries"[95] of the prince, and of their tenures. For instance, Alfonso de Stapulia and Davillo de Bernardia held the arch-dukedoms of Stapulia and Bernardia under the Prince of Purpoole, with the right to "relieve all wants and wrongs of all ladies, matrons, and maids," and to render "on the day of his Excellency's coronation, a coronet of gold, and yearly five hundred millions sterling." Cornelius Combaldus held the grange of Tottenham "in free and common soccage, by the twenty-fourth part of a night's fee and by rendring to the Master of the Wardrobe so many cunny furr as will serve to line his night-cap, and face a pair of mittins; and yielding yearly four quarters of rye, and threescore double duckets on the feast of St. Pancras."[96]

The Prince of Purpoole, simulating the sovereign of England, then issued a holiday pardon to all criminals, much as the president of the United States sometimes remits federal prisoners at Christmas. The puns in the use of legal terminology and the numerous exceptions which render the pardon nugatory are so amusing that it is quoted:

In tender regard, and gracious consideration of the humble affection of our loyal lords and subjects; and by understanding that by often violating of laudable customs, prescriptions, and laws, divers have incurred inevitable and incurable dangers of lands, goods, life, and members, if it be not by our clemency redressed, respected, and pardoned: We therefore, hoping for better obedience and observation of our said laws and customs, do grant and publish this our General and Free Pardon of all dangers, pains, penalties, forfeitures or offences, whereunto and wherewith they are now charged, or chargeable, by reason of mis-government, mis-demeanour, mis-behaviour, or fault, either of commission, omission, or otherwise howsoever or whatsoever.

It is therefore Our will and pleasure, that all and every public person and persons, whether they be strangers or naturals, within Our dominions, be by virtue hereof excused, suspended, and dis-

[95] Feudaries.

[96] Nichols, *Elizabeth,* III, 269–270.

charged from all and all manner of treasons, contempts, offences, trespasses, forcible entries, intrusions, disseisins, torts, wrongs, injuries, over-throws, over-thwartings, cross-bitings, coney-catchings, frauds, conclusions, fictions, fractions, fashions, fancies, or ostentations: also all and all manner of errors, misprisions, mistakings, overtakings, double dealings, combinations, confederacies, conjunctions, oppositions, interpositions, suppositions, and suppositaries: also all and all manner of intermedlance or medlance, privy-searches, routs and riots, incombrances, pluralities, formalities, deformalities, disturbances, duplicities, jeofails in insufficiencies or defects: also all and all manner of sorceries, inchantments, conjurations, spells, or charms: all destruction, obstructions, and constructions: all evasions, invashions, charges, surcharges, discharges, commands, countermands, checks, counterchecks, and counterbuffs: also all and all manner of inhibitions, prohibitions, insurrections, corrections, conspiracies, concavities, coinings, superfluities, washings, clippings, and shavings: all and all manner of multiplications, inanities, installations, destillations, constillations, necromancies, and incantations: all and all manner of mis-feasance, non-feasance, or too much feasance: all attempts or adventures, skirmages, assaults, grapplings, closings, or encounters: all mis-prisonments, or restraints of body or member: and all and all manner of pains and penalties personal or pecuniary whatsoever, committed, made, or done, against our crown and dignity, peace, prerogatives, laws, and customs, which shall not herein hereafter be in some sort expressed, mentioned, intended, or excepted.

Except, and always fore-prized out of this General and Free Pardon, all and every such person and persons as shall imagine, think, suppose, or speak and utter any false, seditious, ignominious, or slanderous words, reports, rumours, or opinions, against the dignity, or his Excellency's honourable actions, counsels, consultations, or state of the Prince, his court, counsellors, nobles, knights, and officers.

Except, all such persons as now or hereafter shall be advanced, admitted, or induced to any corporal or personal benefice, administration, charge, or cure, of any manner of personage, and shall not be personally resident, commorant, or incumbent in, at, or upon the whole, or some part or parcel of the said benefice, administration, or cure; but absent himself wilfully or negligently, by the space of four-score days, nights, or hours, and not having any special substituted, instituted, or inducted Vicar, incumbant, or concumbent, daily, or any other time, duly to express, enjoy and supply his absence, room, or vacation.

Except, all such persons as have, or shall have any charge, occasion, chance, opportunity, or possible means to entertain, serve, recreate, delight, or discourse, with any vertuous or honourable lady, or gentlewoman, matron, or maid, publicly, privately, or familiarly, and shall faint, fail, or be deemed to faint or fail in courage, or countenance, semblance, gesture, voice, speech, or attempt, or in act or adventure, or in any other matter, thing, manner, mystery, or accomplishment, due, decent, or appertinent to her or their honour, dignity, desert, expectation, desire, affection, inclination, allowance, or acceptance; to be daunted, dismayed, or to stand mute, idle, frivolous or defective, or otherwise dull, contrary, sullen, malcontent, melancholy, or different from the profession, practice, and perfection, of a compleat and consummate gentleman or courtier.

Except, all such persons as by any force, or fraud, and dissimulation, shall procure, be it by letters, promises, messages, contracts, and other inveaglings, any lady or gentlewoman, woman or maid, sole or covert, into his possession or convoy, and shall convey her into any place where she is or shall be of full power and opportunity to bargain, give, take, buy, sell, or change; and shall suffer her to escape, and return at large, without any such bargain, sale, gift, or exchange performed and made, contrary to former expected, expressed, employed contract or consent.

Except, all such persons as by any slander, libel, word, or note, bewray, betray, defame, or suffer to be defamed, any woman, wife, widow, or maid, in whose affairs, secrets, suits, services, causes, actions, or other occupations, he hath been at any time conversant, employed, or trained in, or admitted unto, contrary to his plighted promise, duty, and allegiance; and to the utter disparagement of others hereafter to be received, retained, embraced, or liked in like services, performances, or advancements.

Except, all intrusions and forcible entries had, made, or done, into or upon any of the Prince's widows, or wards female, without special licence; and all fines passed for the same.

Except, all concealed fools, idiots, and madmen that have not to this present sued forth any livery of their wits, nor *ouster le mayne* of their senses, until the Prince have had primer seisin thereof.

Except, all such persons as, for their lucre and gain of living, do keep or maintain, or else frequent and resort unto, any common house, alley, open or privy place of unlawful exercises; as of vaulting, bowling, or any forbidden manner of shooting, as at pricks in common highways, ways of sufferance or ease to market-towns or fairs, or at short butts, not being of sufficient length and distance, or at any roving or unconstant mark, or that shoot any shafts, arrows, or bolts, of unseasonable wood or substances, or without an head, or of too short and small size, contrary to the customs, laws, and statutes, in such cases made and provided.

Except, all such persons as shall put or cast into any waters, salt or fresh, or any brooks, brinks, chinks, pits, pools, or ponds, any snare, or other engine, to danger or destroy the fry or breed of any young lampreys, boards, loaches, bullheads, cods, whitings, pikes, ruffs, or pearches, or any other young store of spawns or fries, in any flood-gate, sluice, pipe, or tail of a mill, or any other streight stream, brook, or river, salt or fresh; the same fish being then of insufficiency in age and quantity, or at that time not in convenient season to be used and taken.

Except, all such persons as shall hunt in the night, or pursue any bucks or does; or with painted faces, vizards, or other disguisings, in the day-time; or any such as do wrongfully and unlawfully, without consent or leave given or granted, by day or by night, break or enter into any park impailed, or other several close, inclosure, chace, or purliew, inclosed or compassed with wall, pale, grove, hedge, or bushes, used still and occupied for the keeping, breeding, or cherishing of young deer, prickets, or any other game, fit to be preserved and nourished; or such as do hunt, chase, or drive out any such deer, to the prejudice and decay of such game and pass-times within our dominions.

Except, all such persons as shall shoot in any hand gun, demy-hag, or hag butt, either halfshot, or bullet, any fowl, bird, or beast; either at any deer, red or fallow, or any other thing or things, except it be a butt set, laid, or raised in some convenient place, fit for the same purpose.

Except, all and every artificer, crafts-man, labourer, householder, or servant, being a layman, which hath not lands to the yearly value of forty shillings; or any clerk, not admitted or advanced to the benefice of the value of ten pounds *per annum*, that with any greyhound, mongrel, mastiff, spaniel, or other dogs, doth hunt in other men's parks, warrens, and coney-grees; or use any ferrets, hare-pipes, snarles, ginns, or other knacks or devises, to take or destroy does, hares, or coneys, or other gentlemen's game, contrary to the form and meaning of a statute in that case provided.

Except, all merchant-adventurers, that ship or lade any wares or merchandize, into any port or creek, in any Flemish, French, or Dutch, or other outlandish hoy, ship, or bottom, whereof the Prince, nor some of his subjects, be not possessioners and proprietaries; and the masters and mariners of the same vessels and bottoms to be the Prince's subjects; whereby our own shipping is many times unfraught, contrary unto divers statutes in that case provided.

Except, all owners, masters and pursers of our ships, as, for the transportation of freight from one port to another, have received and taken any sums of money above the statute-allowance in that behalf, *viz.*, for every dry fatt, 6*d.*; for every bale, one foot long, 1*s.*; for every hogshead, pipe, or tierce of wine, 5*s*.

Except, all decayed houses of husbandry, and housewifery, and inclosures, and severalties, converting of any lands used and occupied to tillage and sowing, into pasture and feeding whereby idleness increaseth, husbandry and housewifery is decayed, and towns are dis-peopled, contrary to the statute in that case made and provided.

Except, all such persons as shall maliciously and wilfully burn or cut, or cause to be burned or cut, any conduit, or trough, pipe, or any other instrument used as a means of conveyance of any liquor, water, or other kind of moisture.

Except, all commoners within any forest, chace, moor, marsh, heath, or other waste ground, which hath put to pasture into, or upon the same, any stoned horses, not being of the altitude and height contained in the statute in that case made and provided for the good breed of strong and large horses, which is much decayed; little stoned horses, nags, and hobbies, being put to pasture there, and in such commons.

Except, all fugitives, failers, and flinchers, that with shame and discredit are fled and vanished out of the Prince's dominions of

Purpoole, and especially from his Court at *Graya*, this time of *Christmas*, to withdraw themselves from his Honour's service and attendance, contrary to their duty and allegiance, and to their perpetual ignominy, and incurable loss of credit and good opinion, which belongeth to ingenuous and wellminded gentlemen.

Except, all concealments, and wrongful detainments of any subsidies and revenues, benevolences, and receipts upon privy seals, &c.

Except, all, and all manner of offences, pains, penalties, mulcts, fines, amerciaments, and punishments, corporal and pecuniary, whatsoever.

The pensioners and the attendants, led by the master of the revels, then entertained his Highness with galliards and other old measures. The success of this first grand night was so phenomenal and the number of guests so extraordinary that similar grand nights were observed.

On Innocents night, amid a multitude of "lords, ladies, and worshipful personages," the ambassador of Frederick Templarius, emperor of the Inner Temple, arrived with portfolio and train. With loud blasts of the trumpet, he was conducted to the presence of his Highness, by whose side he was placed. The ambassador then conveyed the salutation of Frederick Templarius to the prince, whose renown "was not contained within the bounds of the Ocean," to which the prince made gracious reply, emphasizing the amicable relationship which had long existed between the two houses. At this time, however, great tumult arose: "worshipful personages" and "gentlewomen whose sex did privilege them from violence" could not be removed from the stage. Therefore, the entertainment arranged for the ambassador could not be presented; he and his suite, hence, retired in dudgeon. After this,

it was thought good not to offer any thing of account, saving dancing and revelling with gentlewomen; and after such sports, a Comedy of Errors (like to Plautus his Menechmus) was played by the players. So that night was begun and continued to the end in nothing but confusion and errors; whereupon, it was ever afterwards called, "The Night of Errors."[97]

Concerning the presentation of the *Comedy of Errors*, Francis Bacon's chief biographer says: "This performance seems to have been regarded as the crowning disgrace of this unfortunate Grand Night; a fact, by the way, indicating (if it were Shakespeare's play, as I suppose it was) either rich times or poor tastes."[98] This *contretemps*, however, gave rise to amusing improvised entertainment for the next night, December 29, at which time a commission of oyer and terminer was directed to members of his Highness' council, ordering them to inquire into the cause of the disorder. On the subsequent night "a sorcerer or conjurer" was charged with rearing scaffolds to the top of the house and inviting guests to the sports, only to foist "a company of base and common fellows, to make up our disorders with a play of Errors and Confusions."[99] The prisoner, who was tried before a jury of twenty-four gentlemen, offered, through the master of the requests, the defense that those hurly-burlies which the gentlemen thought that they had witnessed were "but vain illusions, fancies, dreams, and enchantments." The accused then made countercharge of negligence and misgovernment against the officers of the law. The prisoner was acquitted, whereas the attorney, solicitor, and master of the requests were committed to the charge of the lieutenant of the tower.

On January 3, after precaution had been taken to prevent tumult, a great company was invited to the revels,[100] at which

[97] Nichols, *Elizabeth*, III, 279. *Gesta Grayorum*, pp. 30–31.

[98] Spedding, I, 325–343. *Twelfth Night* was performed in the Middle Temple Hall in 1601 (Bedwell, p. 51).

[99] Nichols, *Elizabeth*, III, 280.

[100] "The Right Honourable the Lord Keeper, the Earls of Shrewsbury, Cumberland, Northumberland, Southampton, and Essex; the Lords Buckhurst, Windsor, Mountjoy, Sheffield, Compton, Rich, Burleygh, Mounteagle, and the Lord Thomas Howard; Sir Thomas Henneage, Sir Robert Cecill" (*ibid.*, p. 281).

time the gentlemen of Gray's determined to repair their lost honor. After "a variety of musick," the following device, one of the early approaches to the masque, was presented: the Goddess of Amity was seated upon an altar, attended by her arch-flamen and other servants, besides nymphs and fairies, who sang and played on viols hymns of praise to the goddess; then many of the classical friends, Theseus and Perithous, Achilles and Patroclus, Pylades and Orestes, and Scipio and Lelius, offered incense before the goddess. Finally Graius and Templarius came, arm in arm, and burnt incense, but there was "troubled smoak, and dark vapour, that choaked the flame, and smothered the clear burning thereof."[101] However, after the arch-flamen had performed "mystical ceremonies and invocations" and after the nymphs had sung "hymns of pacification," the flame burned bright, and Graius and Templarius were pronounced perpetual friends. The prince then made the ambassador a knight of the helmet. After congratulatory speeches, the king at arms read the articles of the order, which provided, among other things, that no knight should resort "to any grammar-rules," that every knight should "perform all requisite and manly service, be it night-service, or otherwise, as the case requireth, to all ladies and gentlewomen, beautiful by nature or by art," that each knight should wear three colors for each mistress, that he should read "Guizo, the French Academy, Galiatto the Courtier, Plutarch, the Arcadia, and the Neoterical Writers" and should "frequent the Theatre, and such like places of experience," and he should yield "all homage, loyalty, unaffected admiration and all humble service . . . to the incomparable Empress of the Fortunate Island."[102]

After a banquet, the prince called upon six of the lords of his privy council for advice concerning a program of action

[101] *Ibid.*, p. 282.

[102] *Ibid.*, p. 287. Even today the gentlemen of the Inns drink to the immortal memory of Queen Elizabeth.

for the betterment of the state. The address of the prince and the replies of the six councilors (of which Appendix E is comprised), are especially important in that they, like much of the entire entertainment of this Christmas period, are supposed to be the work of Francis Bacon, whose biographer says:

> That the speeches of the six councillors were written by him, and by him alone, no one who is at all familiar with his style either of thought or expression will for a moment doubt. They carry his signature in every sentence. The second and fifth speak out Bacon's true mind and judgment, and are not merely playful. They contain an enumeration of those very reforms in state and government which throughout his life he was most anxious to see realized.[103]

Comparison of the speeches of the six councilors with Bacon's essays, and particularly the sixth speech with "Of Maſques and Triumphs," and with his political theory expressed elsewhere leads to the conclusion that they are the work of Bacon. It is significant, as Spedding[104] notes, that customary travestied legal argot has been supplanted in these speeches by solemnity of style. Ironic is the fact that, on December 5, 1594, Lady Bacon wrote to her son Anthony: "I trust they will not mum nor mask . . . sinfully at Gray's Inn. Who were sometime counted first, God grant they wane not daily, and deserve to be named last."

The gentlemen of Gray's conducted themselves so nobly that Sir John Spencer,[105] the lord mayor of London, invited them to be his dinner guests at Crosby's Place, in Bishopsgate-street, on the following evening. On the way to the

[103] Spedding, I, 325–343. [104] *Supra.*

[105] At about this time, but probably a bit later rather than earlier, Lord Compton of Gray's Inn eloped with Sir John's daughter, whom he conveyed, with no lordly gesture but in true Falstaffian manner, in a baker's basket. Through mediation of Elizabeth, "Rich Spencer" was so much reconciled to the marriage that he bequeathed to his daughter half a million pounds, a fortune which is said to have "turned the head, and even the brain, of . . . Compton" (Barton, p. 191).

mayor's house, where a costly dinner was served and where there was a variety of music and gay reveling, the prince and the ambassador were preceded by their suites, to the number of eighty gentlemen, all of whom were mounted. The gentlemen of Gray's Inn wore white feathers, and the gentlemen of the Inner Temple ash-colored feathers.

On Twelfth Night, another masque-like celebration was held. Six knights of the helmet entered the hall with three prisoners "attired like monsters and miscreants." The knights, returning from an expedition in succor of the emperor of Russia against the Tartars, captured the three prisoners, Envy, Malcontent, and Folly, as they were conspiring against the prince. After two goddesses, Virtue and Amity, had covenanted to protect the prince against all enemies, the prisoners were transported. Thereupon, the six knights, followed by other gentlemen and ladies, enjoyed galliards. Preceded by a blare of trumpets, the ambassador of the emperor of Russia and Muscovy entered with letters of credence. He commended especially the gallantry of the six knights, and requested that the prince send to his lord a company of one hundred similar knights for combat against the Tartars. When the petition had been granted, a "running banquet," accompanied by music, was served.

A postboy then entered with letters concerning conditions in various parts of the state. One such letter from Knightsbridge advised that three foreigners, with letters of reprisal, were despoiling the realm. Besides these strangers, named Johannes Shagbag,[106] Robertus Untruss, James Rapax, alias Capax, various former soldiers, maimed in wars against the Amazons, and beggars were said to be committing depredations. Another letter, written at sea and directed to the lord admiral, advised that an armada of French Amazons was working great injury along the coast. After a burlesque of

[106] Attempt has been made to consider this a reference to Shakespeare.

trading with the Netherlands, the rest of the letter is devoted to a comparison, by innuendo, of the conduct of a ship in battle to human physiological functions. Similar letters gave intelligence of rebellious and insurrectionary conspiracies in Stapulia and Bernardia.[107] But the prince, in his concluding speech, said that he was not to be dispirited by wars and rumors of wars; but that insurrections are like mushrooms, "sprung up in a night, and rotten before the morning."[108] Congratulating himself upon the esteem in which he was held by foreign emperors, he prepared his knights for an expedition against the Tartars, and urged the ladies to be benign to those who undertook hard adventures for them. After dancing, the company left.

On the next morning the prince departed for Russia, where he remained until Candlemas. Great plans were made for his triumphal return, but the governors forbade rearing scaffolds again in the hall. Nevertheless, on January 28, while the gentlemen of Gray's sat at dinner, the king at arms, following a trumpet blast, announced the approach of his Highness with his retinue aboard fifteen barges, gaily decorated with streamers and banners. At the foot of the stairs at Greenwich, ordnance was fired. The prince, however, apologized for not making a call upon her Majesty and kissing her sacred hands, but promised to return at Shrovetide, if his health then permitted. Elizabeth graciously replied that "she liked well his gallant shews, that were made at his triumphant return," and promised to afford him entertainment at Shrovetide; moreover, she commanded the lieutenant of the Tower to welcome him "with a volley of great ordnance"[109] at Tower-hill, where a hundred horsemen awaited his return. At St. Paul's School, where his Highness and his entourage stopped, one of the students delivered a welcoming oration in Latin. Finally, the prince

[107] Staple Inn and Barnard's Inn.

[108] Nichols, *Elizabeth,* III, 304. [109] *Ibid.,* p. 307.

arrived at his court, where he was greeted with salute of ordnance and blare of trumpets.

The celebration of the Christmas of 1594–95 by the gentlemen of Gray's Inn continued until Shrovetide, at which time a masque[110] was presented for the diversion of her Majesty.

Much like the Gray's Inn entertainment of 1594–95 was that of the Middle Temple of 1599,[111] an account of which is contained in an interesting pamphlet which bears the following title-page:

Le Prince d'Amour,
OR THE
Prince of Love
WITH A
COLLECTION
Of Several Ingenious
Poems
and
SONGS
By the Wits of the Age
London
Printed for William Leake at the Crown in
Fleet-ſtreet, betwixt the two Temple Gates, 1660.[112]

This interesting document, which has been overlooked by historians of the Temple, is attributed by Bodleian Library to Benjamin Ruddierd (Rudyerd), largely because the latter section, which was evidently published separately under the title, "A Brief Chronicle of the Dark Raigne of the bright Prince of Burning Love," bears the initials "R. W."[113] The masque mentioned in this section is ordinarily considered to

110 *The Masque of Proteus.*

111 Chambers, *Med.*, I, 416.

112 A copy of this pamphlet may be found in the Treasure Room of Widener Library.

113 Chambers (*Med.*, I, 416) has taken cognizance of the masque noted in the last section of this pamphlet, as has Steele, who, under date of "January 6, 1597–8?" quotes a description by Sir Benjamin Rudyerd in *Noctes Templariae.*

have been presented at Whitehall in 1599–1600, because the "Brief Chronicle" is dated "*Ano ab Aula condita* the 27," and the Middle Temple hall, in which most of the entertainment was produced, was built in 1572. As the court was at Richmond at this season, there is much confusion as to the date.[114] While it is thought that the body of *Le Prince d'Amour* is of the same date as the section entitled "A Brief Chronicle," this fact may not be established definitively. In any event, *Le Prince d'Amour* is patently a description of a typical Christmas entertainment at the Middle Temple. The dedication of this pamphlet, "To the Honourable the Society of the Middle-Temple," is signed "W. L.," apparently being the initials of William Leake, the printer, who says that the prince has returned to the society which created him, that the members of 1660 might "look on paſt innocent and ingenious pleaſures and divertiſements wherewith your Honourable Society uſed to entertain it ſelf," these entertainments being the glory of all England. The Prince d'Amour is also

Palſgrave of *Hartſbroken*, Duke of *Suſpircia*, Marqueſs of *Braineſwound*, Governor of *Florida* and *Exultantia*, Great Commander of all the Seas from the Streights of *Genua* to the Bay of *Porto deſiderato*, and chief General of all *Venus* forces, from *Iapanto* to *Quevera* by the Weſt, and from *Rio des Amazones* to *Lapland* by the North; in all people and Nations that underſtand the language of Seeing and Feeling.

The titles of the prince are then explained, followed by emblazonment of his arms. The champion of the prince then laments the fact that the descendants of the Knights Templars have forsaken chivalry and love: none has sighed, none has frequented public shows, and none has courted the door of his mistress on a cold winter's night, but all have led lives of ease and venery. The champion then throws his "Gantlet"

[114] Steele, "January 6, 1597–8?."

on the ground as a symbol of his readiness to defend his assertion. Then the duties of the various officers of the prince are assigned: The lord president is to make proclamation that "any Gentlewoman being taken in the Armes of any Gentleman, be presumed to be his Sister, or his Cousin at the least, and that she be presumed to be no better than swowning and he striving to put life into her." The arch-flamen is to "dispense and Canonize," and "allow Pluralities in Love" to those whom nature has specially graced. The lord chamberlain is to keep "all Roomes . . . sweetly perfumed" and see that the windows admit only twilight, "to cover Blemishes." The master of the revels is to see that "no Gentlemans Voice drown the base Viol." In like manner, the lord chancellor, the lord marshal, the lord treasurer, the master of the horse, the lord president of the province of New Inn, the lord admiral, the lord privy seal, Lord Saint George, the Comptroller, the secretary, the lord chief baron, the captain of the guard, the lieutenant of the Tower, the captain of the "Seraglia," and the herald are assigned duties which are conducive to social intercourse. This is followed by a prognostication, a description of the wearing apparel of each of the officers, a speech by the prince's orator, called the "Tufftaffata Speech," and an extemporaneous reply by the clerk of the council, called "The Fustian Answer." The prince then creates a new order, called the "Knights of the *Quiver*." After various proclamations and trumpet soundings, the herald reads the articles of the order, including the following: "24. Item, That he learn no speeches out of Playes to entertain the time; and that his Picture be not drawn in clothes transgressing the Statute of Apparel. . . ." This is followed by congees and oaths of office. Then a mock court is held, in which Jealousy is charged with sedition. A grand jury of twenty-four gentlemen with fanciful, sensual names is impaneled, and charged with the duty of adjudging the defendant, who is alleged to have shifted his mistress more frequently than his wearing apparel. The prisoner pleads not guilty, and requests trial by the laws of Love and inquest by true lovers. After the criminal code is interpreted for the grand jury, a petit jury, composed of gentlemen bearing names well known in amorous argot, is impaneled. The chief justice, in charging the latter jury, says "6. If any man kiſs the ſeat of his Miſtrſſes ſaddle . . . whereon she hath ſitten, he ſhall be taken as a vain worſhipper of Idols." The clerk of the crown then reads to the jury the notes that he has taken of the condemnatory speech of the prince's attorney, which proves to be a series of salacious verses. Jealousy, being found guilty of sedition in the kingdom of Love, is sentenced to imprisonment in the "most loathsome dungeon of the Fort of Fancy." The prince, Sir Martino, and a buffoon, Milorsius Stradilax, are among the principal characters of this entertainment.

The Christmas celebration of 1628–29 of the Middle Temple is described by the biographer[115] of Bulstrode Whitelocke, who was master of the revels. The entertainment was inaugurated with nightly gatherings in the large room, called the "Oracle of Apollo," of Saint Dunstan's tavern, where a miniature parliament was held, followed by dinner and supper. On All-hallows day, the master was attended by sixteen handsome dancers, each richly clothed, who "flaunted through galliards, corantos, French and country dances." The perfection of this dancing attracted ladies and gentlemen of the court, and even a famous German lord, then being lionized in London, who avowed that "dere was no such nople gollege in Ghristendom as deir's."[116]

One of the Evelyn analects describes the Christmas diversion at Lincoln's Inn, as follows:

[115] R. H. Whitelocke, *Memoirs, Biographical and Historical, of Bulstrode Whitelocke.*

[116] *Ibid.*, p. 57.

1661–2 1st January: I went to London, invited to the solemn foolery of the Prince de la Grange, at Lincoln's Inn, where came the King, Duke, etc. It began with a grand masque, and a formal pleading before the mock Princes, Grandees, Nobles, and Knights of the Sun. He had his Lord Chancellor, Chamberlain, Treasurer, and other Royal Officers, gloriously clad and attended. It ended in a magnificent banquet. One Mr. Lort was the young spark who maintained the pageantry.[117]

Evelyn says, further, that exactly twenty years before he was one of the comptrollers of the Middle Temple Christmas revelers, at which time the holiday was "kept with great solemnity."[118]

From a contemporary manuscript, we learn that Charles, his queen, and the Prince of Orange were present *incognito* at the Temple revels in early December, 1670, and on January 27, 1671; and at Lincoln's Inn revels on January 28, 1671, when the Duke of Somerset, the Duke of Richmond and Gordon, and the Marquis of Worcester joined the party. At this time, Mr. Rich, master of the revels of Lincoln's Inn, was knighted.[119]

The Christmas of 1697 was observed at the Inner Temple with much ceremonial. On January 21, 1698, distinguished guests, including the Czar of Muscovy, who later became known as Peter the Great, were beguiled with a masquerade. Peter was strikingly costumed as a butcher. The king was so well pleased that he returned on February 26 to participate in another masquerade.[120]

Besides masquerades, regular plays were presented at the

[117] Concerning this merrymaking, Pepys says, "To Faithorne's, . . . and comes by the King's life-guard, he being gone to Lincoln's Inn this afternoon to see the Revels there; there being, according to an old custom, a prince and all his nobles, and other matters of sport and charge" (January 3, 1662).

[118] *Diary*, December 15, 1641.

[119] Black Book, III, 451, quoting MSS. of H. S. Le Fleming, Esq.; Hist. MSS. Com. 12th Rep., App. VII, p. 75.

[120] Luttrell, *Brief Relation*, IV, 335–349; Williamson, p. 661.

Inns during the Christmas holidays as a part of the entertainment. As early as 1509, the Middle Temple paid the players (*ludatores*) six shillings, eight pence.[121] Various allowances were made by other Inns to many companies, including the boys of the Queen's Chapel and Lord Roche's players.[122]

During the early sixteenth century, riots, proceeding chiefly from gambling, had caused vexation to the governors of the Inner Temple. As early as 1521,[123] and again in 1532,[124] gambling was peremptorily prohibited within the house, no exception being made for the holidays. In 1561,[125] another mandate was promulgated specifically placing the Christmas holiday within the prohibition. In 1609, the Middle Temple prohibited dicing at Christmas.[126] On the whole, however, these attempts to regulate gambling seem to have been sporadic, and to have been aimed at the introduction of undesirable strangers, for on November 27, 1614, the Inner Temple ordered that none should play at dice "except he be a gentleman of the same society and in commons."[127] In the fourth year of the reign of Charles I (1629), Gray's Inn forbade gambling except during the twenty days in Christmas.[128] In 1639–40, the tumult became so great at the Inner Temple that the benchers forbade keeping of Christmas commons, declaring the disorder to be

> to the greate offence of Almighty God the dishonor and scandall of this Society, the most dangerous infection and corruption of the civill company and the members thereof and the manifest prejudice

[121] Middle Temple Records, p. 30. [122] Bellot, pp. 1–3.

[123] "Order that none of the society shall play within the Inn at the game called 'shoffe boorde' or 'slypgrote,' under the penalty of 6s. 8d." (Inderwick, I, 63).

[124] "Order that none of the society shall play at the game called 'shobebord,' nor at dice or cards within the House of the Temple under penalty of 3s. 4d. each" (*ibid.*, p. 100).

[125] *Ibid.*, p. 211. [126] Hopwood, year 1609.

[127] Inderwick, II, 83–84. [128] Dawson, p. 201.

of the House in divers respects tending to the ruine and subversion thereof if it be not timely prevented.[129]

When the doors of the hall and kitchen were locked, the gentlemen, with drawn swords, broke them open, and, after appointing officers, kept Christmas as usual. By order of his Majesty, they were later commanded to desist from their celebration. In their remonstrance to the Council of State, the young gentlemen, smug as new-licked pups, exercised their embryonic powers of debate as follows:

In the keeping of this Christmas we conceive that we have not offended or brought in any innovation, or permitted the least disorder whereby our Christmas should be suppressed, or our ancient privilege taken from us to be transferred to other Houses, Gray's Inn and Lincoln's Inn having since we desisted, permitted the very same company to play in both Houses, so that the reformation aimed at is no ways redressed. We further declare that many well affected persons of our society, being sensible of the general inconvenience, have endeavoured a sudden reformation, but which we, upon mature consideration, found impossible to be done any other way than by debarring of all manner of play at dice in our hall; and because we conceived music could not be paid for, nor our butlers rewarded and our other expenses of entertainment defrayed, without excessive charge to the gentlemen in commons, therefore conceived it fit to allow of play of dice in the libraries, provided none but such as were invited or well known to some gentlemen of our house should be admitted to play, and this order being punctually observed would redress the disorder complained of, which reformation had been put in execution this Christmas but for the reasons here stated.[130]

Legally considered, this argument is fallacious; it is, however, very ingenious economically.

Things continued to grow worse. Evelyn, whose heart Christian zeal was devouring, as the vulture consumed the

[129] Williamson, pp. 360–361, quoting A. P., III, 19.

[130] Calendar of State Papers, Domestic, 1639–40, pp. 304–305, quoted by Inderwick, II, Appendix X.

liver of Tityus, lamented the great amount of play at the Middle Temple in 1642; in 1668, he spoke of the Christmas entertainment at the same house as being "an old riotous custom" having relation "neither to virtue nor policy."[131] Hurly-burly must have been prevalent during this holiday season, for even the indolent moral sense of Pepys became animated:

> I . . . stepped into the two Temple halls, and there saw the dirty 'prentices and idle people playing; wherein I was mistaken in thinking to have seen gentlemen of quality playing there, as I think it was when I was a little child . . . one cursing and swearing, and another muttering and grumbling to himself; to see how the dice will run good luck in one hand, for half an hour together, and another have no good luck at all; to see how easily . . . a £100 is won or lost; to see two or three gentlemen come in there drunk; to see the different humours of the gamesters, when it is bad, how ceremonious they are to call for new dice, to shift their places, to alter their manner of throwing; to see how persons of the best quality do here sit down, and play with people of any, though meaner.[132]

Concerning dicing at Christmas, Sir Simonds d'Ewes[133] says:

> At the said Temple[134] was a lieutenant chosen and much gaming and other excesses increased, during these festival days, by his residing and keeping a standing table there. When sometimes I turned in thither to behold their sports, and saw the many oaths, execrations, and quarrels that accompanied their design, I began seriously to loathe it, though, at the time, I conceived the sport itself to be lawful.

Again in 1696, Evelyn speaks of "a riotous and revelling Christmas, according to custom" at the Inner Temple.[135]

It was long felt at the various Inns that plays as well as dicing, led to debauchery. In 1551, it was ordered at Gray's

[131] *Diary*, January 9, 1668.
[132] *Ibid.*, January 1, 1668.
[133] *Autobiography*, p. 161.
[134] Middle Temple.
[135] *Diary*, December 12, 1696–97.

Inn that there should "be no Comedies, called Interludes, in this Houſe, out of Term times, but when the Feaſt of the Nativity of our Lord is ſolemnly obſerved."[136] In 1611, the parliament of the same house provided

> for that great disorder and scurrility is brought into this House by lewd and lascivious plays, it is likewise ordered in this parliament that from henceforth there shall be no more plays in this House, either upon the feast of All Saints or Candlemas day, but the same from henceforth to be utterly taken away and abolished.[137]

The gentlemen of the Middle Temple were often in such a ferment during Christmas celebrations that they made outcry at night and broke open doors. Various restraining ordinances[138] were enacted, which appear, however, to have been inefficacious. In 1590, Lower was expelled for using "reproachfull and contemptuous words"[139] to a bencher who attempted to expostulate with him. During the following year students and townsfolk, disguised, again committed acts of vandalism.

Nocturnal bombardment was one of the chief causes of consternation of the benchers, and apparently of the court. A peal of ordnance of the Lincoln's revelers in 1622–23, after a splendid feast, put the city in panic;[140] at about the same time, the lieutenant of the Middle Temple, with thirty of the most gallant of the gentlemen, drank to the health of Lady Elizabeth,[141] each gentleman solemnly kissing his sword and swearing to die in her service, if necessary. The gentlemen, to make a dramatic end of this Christmas, in the middle of Twelfth Night, discharged numerous cannon, which

[136] Dugdale, pp. 285–286; 4 Edward VI, November 17.

[137] Inderwick, II, 56, Parliament of February 10, 1610–11.

[138] Williamson, pp. 212–213. [139] *Ibid.*

[140] Nichols, *James*, IV, 803; see p. 752 for a similar story of the preceding Christmas celebration at Gray's Inn.

[141] Lady Elizabeth became the Queen of Bohemia. The masque prepared for her marriage will be considered later.

they had conveyed from the Tower in four carts; it is said that the king, having been awakened, shouted "Treason! Treason!" whereupon the Earl of Arundel ran to his chamber, with sword gleaming, to be the protector of the princely person.[142] It may be conjectured that this celebration was not so successful politically for the young men as it might have been. In 1627, Mr. Palmer, the Templars' lord of misrule, set out, on Twelfth eve, to collect his annual revenues in Ram Alley and in Fleet Street. That there might be no controversy in the collection of five shillings at each house, the lord was reënforced by a gunner, "a robustious Vulcan," who carried, instead of a gun, a tremendous smith's hammer. The mayor, getting word of the anvil chorus, decided to vanquish the Titans; he, therefore, with innumerable warders armed with swords, approached the Temple gate, where he demanded the presence of the prince. But the mayor's sally was impotent, for the prince sent an ambassador to advise him that a lord should never deign to leave his court at the request of a mere mayor. The mayor, who had expected a prompt effluence, finally agreed with vexation to meet the prince half way. Accepting this compromise, the prince advanced, but he declined to remove his hat, whereupon the air close to his ears was cut by the mayor's halberdiers. The lord, finding himself truly a lord of misrule, was forced to the ground. He was then placed in prison, where he remained for two nights, during which time much of his glory vanished. Through the interposition of the king's attorney, the lord was finally released after he had agreed to make restitution to his involuntary tenants. The two disputants were then transported in the coach of the attorney-general to the court, where the king joined their hands in reconciliation.[143]

[142] Birch, *James I*, II, 359–360, quoting letter of January 25, 1622–23 from the Rev. Mr. Joseph Mead to Sir Martin Stuteville.

[143] Letters of Mr. Joseph Mead to Sir Martin Stuteville, from Harleian MSS. Vol. CCCXC, fols., 339, 343. Letters of January 12 and 19, 1627, quoted by Dawson, pp. 198–199, and Williamson, pp. 360–361.

The history of the Inns is filled with escapades, insurrections,[144] and reconciliations.

As early as 1580, regulations were enacted at the Inner Temple against the turbulence at Christmas. In 1628, it was provided that strangers should not be admitted to commons, and that there should be no "drinking of healths."[145] By 1631, Christmas celebrations had become so riotous that the following orders were agreed upon:

1. That Christmas commons shall continue by the space of three weeks only and no longer, according to the ancient usage and custom of this House.
2. That every week there be three stewards chosen for that week, according to the old order of Christmas, and the innovation of treasurers to be abolished. . . .
5. That no stranger nor any of this society that hath not been in the ordinary commons of this House within two years . . . shall be admitted . . . in commons in the time of Christmas.
6. That there be no allowance of wine, but only "one pottle" to the steward's mess, according to the ancient usage of Christmas.
7. That there be no drinking of healths, nor any wine or tobacco uttered or sold within the House.
8. That there shall not be any knocking with boxes or calling aloud for gamesters.
9. That no play shall be continued within the House upon any Saturday night or upon Christmas even, at night, after twelve of the clock.
10. That there shall not be any going abroad out of the circuit of this House or without any of the gates, by any lord or other gentleman, to break open any house or chamber or to take anything in the name of rent or a distress.
11. That for preventing of quarrels within the House and that general scandal and obliquy which the House hath heretofore incurred in time of Christmas, there shall no gentleman of this House side with any person whatsoever that shall offer to disturb the peace

[144] Pepys, *Diary* (May 19, 1667), speaks of rebellion at Gray's.
[145] Inderwick, II, Introduction, lxxviii.

and quiet of the House, but shall endeavour to punish them according to the old custom of the House, and that no strangers be suffered to come within the hall, but only such as shall appear and seem to be of good sort and fashion.[146]

In 1634, because of the plague, no commons was kept.[147] In 1639, illegal commons, heretofore noted, was held.[148] Also in 1661, order was adopted, with the usual preamble, in which Almighty God frowned upon the licentiousness of the Christmas celebration, that commons should be dissolved during the holidays.[149] Similar provision was made in 1664[150] and in 1683.[151]

Thus the magnificence of the Christmas celebration languished, and so languishing did die.

[146] Inderwick, II, 193.
[147] *Ibid.*, Introduction, lxxviii.
[148] *Ibid.*
[149] *Ibid.*, III, 6.
[150] *Ibid.*, p. 30.
[151] *Ibid.*, p. 201.

CHAPTER VI

The Masque

A. THE MASQUE OF 1526

THE transition from the usual boisterous Christmas celebration to that of which the masque constituted the principal form of amusement is best shown in the Saturnalia of 1526 at Gray's Inn. Our sole information concerning this entertainment is found in the *Chronicle*[1] of Hall, who was a member of Gray's. From this account we learn that the celebration was political in its nature, consisting largely of satire of officers of the crown. We may, perhaps, assume that the cause of the imprisonment of the author and one of the actors was the displeasure of Cardinal Wolsey rather than Henry VIII. Of particular importance is the fact that the settings and costumes were colorful and costly, there were plays perhaps by masked actors, and there was dancing. Here, then, meager though the account is, appear all the rudiments of the fully developed masque, prepared for the specific purpose of attacking contemporary political conditions; here appear also the tumult of the ordinary Christmas celebration and survivals of mumming and pageantry. Hall's description of this entertainment follows:

The xviij. Yere of Kyng Henry the viij. This Christmas was a good disguisyng plaied at Greis inne, whiche was compiled for the moste part, by master Ijon Roo seriant at the law. xx. yere past, and long before the Cardinall had any aucthoritie, the effecte of the plaie was, that lord gouernance was ruled by dissipacion and negligence: which caused Rumor Populi, Inward grudge and disdain of wanton souereignetie, to rise with a greate multitude, to expell negligence and dissipacion, and to restore Publik welth again to her estate,

[1] P. 719.

which was so done. This plaie was so set furth with riche and costly apparel, with straunge diuises of Maskes & Morrishes that it was highly praised of all menne, sauyng of the Cardinall, whiche imagined that the plaie had been diuised of hym, & in a greate furie sent for the said master Roo. and toke from hym his Coyfe, and sent him to the Flete, & after he sent for the yong gentlemen, that plaied in the plaie, and them highly rebuked and thretend, & sent one of them called Thomas Moyle of Kent to the Flete, but by the meanes of frendes Master Roo and he wer deliuered at last. This plaie sore displeased the Cardinall, and yet it was neuer meante to hym as you haue harde, wherfore many wisemen grudged to see him take it so hartely, and euere the Cardinall saied that the kyng was highly displeased with it, and spake nothyng of hymself.

B. MASQUES OF 1565–66 AND 1592

COLLIER[2] notes that, in 1565–66, at Shrovetide, the gentlemen of Gray's Inn offered, for the entertainment of Elizabeth, then youthful and gracious,[3] "divers showes," probably including a masque which presented Diana and Pallas.

In 1592–93, Francis Bacon wrote much of the dialogue for a device, probably in the nature of a masque, which, also, was presented before Elizabeth, possibly in connection with an entertainment by Gray's Inn, with which Bacon was long affiliated.[4]

Little information can be obtained concerning these shows, which cannot be established as fully developed masques.

C. THE MASQUE OF PROTEUS

THE Christmas celebration at Gray's Inn during 1594–95, it will be recalled, contained a pageant-like masque, with the

[2] *History of E. D. P.*, I, 191.

[3] Ten years after this, Gerard Legh wrote, "our moſt dreat foueraigne the Queenes maiestie that now is, of whome I pray God, if it be his will, to ſend ſome fruite" (118).

[4] Fleay, *B. C. of the E. D.*, I, 27. Spedding, Bacon's biographer, calls this device *A Conference of Pleasure.*

Goddess of Amity as the chief character, containing setting and dialogue much like the perfected masque. This variegated entertainment was terminated with the presentation before the queen, of a true masque, appropriately called *The Masque of Proteus*, probably on Shrove Tuesday, 1594–95. It is, thus, at the Inns of Court, that the masque was not only developed but also perfected. *The Masque of Proteus*, although it contains no antimasque, has all the qualities of the spectacular masque which became very popular during the early part of the next century.

The Masque of Proteus is usually attributed to Thomas Campion and Francis Davison.[5] In 1602, Davison published the following sonnet on this entertainment:

> Upon presenting her with the Speech at Gray's
> Inn Mask, at the court, 1594,
> Consisting of three parts—the story of *Proteus'*
> Transformations,
> The Wonders of the *Adamantine Rock*, and a
> *Speech* to her Majesty.
>
> Who in these lines may better claim a part,
> That sing the praises of the maiden Queen,
> Than you, fair sweet, that only sovereign been
> Of the poor kingdom of my faithful heart?
> Or, to whose view should I this speech impart;
> Where the adamantine rock's great power is shown;
> But to your conqu'ring eyes, whose force once known,
> Makes even iron hearts loath thence to part?
> Or who of Proteus' sundry transformations,
> May better send you the new feigned story
> Than I, whose love unfeigned felt no mutations,
> Since to be yours I first received the glory?
> Accept then, of these lines, though meanly penned,
> So fit for you to take and me to send.[6]

[5] Brown, pp. vii, viii.

[6] Quoted by Brown, pp. vii–viii.

The principal characters of this masque are Esquire, Proteus, Thamesis, and Amphitrite. The combination of the domestic names "Esquire" and "Thamesis" with the Greek mythological names "Proteus" and "Amphitrite" is significant. Coalescence of folk customs with mythology, of the national with the classical drama is perhaps nowhere more pronounced than in the productions of the Inns of Court. The four main characters are supported by sea nymphs, Tritons, and pygmies.

The masque opens conventionally with a song, said to be the hymn of Campion.[7] After dialogue, in blank verse, between the principal characters, the following compliment is paid to the queen:

> Excellent QUEEN, true Adamant of Hearts;
> Out of that sacred garland ever grew
> Garlands of Virtues, Beauties, and Perfections,
> That Crowns your Crown, and dims your Fortune's beams,
> Vouchsafe some branch, some precious flower, or leaf,
> Which, though it wither in my barren verse.
> May yet suffice to overshade and drown
> The rocks admired of this demy-god.[8]

Then Proteus strikes with his trident[9] on the adamantine rock, which opens, emitting the Christmas prince and his knights in pairs, each couple being followed by pygmies. After dancing a "new devised measure," the gentlemen danced their galliards and courantes with the ladies, while five musicians played. After the pygmies had delivered the escutcheons of the gentlemen to the queen, all the actors reëntered the rock, which closed. The masque was concluded with the singing of another song written by Campion.

After the masque was over, some of the courtiers of the queen danced, whereupon her Majesty exclaimed, "What!

[7] Quoted by Brown, pp. vii-viii. [8] *Gesta Grayorum*, p. 83.
[9] "Bident" in the MS.

shall we have bread and cheese after a banquet?" On the next day, the queen gave to the gentlemen her hand to kiss, and said that Gray's Inn was "an House she was much beholden unto, for that it did always study for some sports to present unto her."[10] On the same night, at the barriers, the Christmas prince won the prize, a jewel containing seventeen diamonds and four rubies, worth a hundred marks. Elizabeth, in tendering the gift to him, said: "That it was not her gift; for if it had, it should have been better; but she gave it him as that prize which was due to his desert and good behaviour in those exercises; and that hereafter he should be remembered with a better reward from herself."[11]

The Masque of Proteus is, then, one of the progenitors of the spectacular masques written and produced by Ben Jonson and Inigo Jones. Thoroughly in the masque tradition are the setting, the mythological characters, the gnomish and choric elements, the opening and closing songs, the accompanying music, the dancing, the use of machinery in unsealing and in shutting the adamantine rock, the rejection of English rhyme for the classical blank verse, the dialogue, and the compliment to the queen. The lack of plot and the unification of the masque through carrying out a theme suggested by the subject are, likewise, in the masque convention. *The Masque of Proteus* was, for some while, the criterion of the occasional masque.

It is probable that Campion and Davison were not consciously imitating French or Italian models nor was it their purpose to re-create the choregraphical drama of the Greeks, or to emulate the *ballet-comique* of Beaujoyeulx. *The Masque of Proteus* is a fusion of various elements of the Greek, Italian, and French drama with thoroughly English material. The gentlemen of Gray's purposed to pay tribute to Elizabeth; for the execution of their design, the authors

[10] *Gesta Grayorum*, p. 87. [11] *Ibid.*, p. 88.

of this masque employed many of the methods of exotic drama, but the product is, on the whole, native.

D. THE MASQUE OF THE NINE PASSIONS

THE last section of *Le Prince d'Amour,*[12] entitled "A Brief Chronicle of the dark Raign of the bright Prince of burning Love," contains not only a description of the buffoon, Milorsius Stradilax, in his "Marmelad-Colour-Taffata Gown," but also a slight account of a masque performed at court during the Christmas celebration of 1599–1600.[13] Part of the account follows: "On Friday, being Twelfth Day, 11 knights and 11 esquires, 9 maskers and 9 torchbearers went to court. . . . When they came to the court, the nine maskers like Paſſions iſſued out of a Heart. All was fortunately performed, and received gracious commendation."[14]

This masque is, therefore, commonly called *A Masque of the Nine Passions.*

E. THE MASQUE OF THE MIDDLE TEMPLE AND LINCOLN'S INN

As both Elizabeth,[15] the daughter of King James I, and the Count Palatine of the Rhine (largely because of his identification with the Protestant movement in Germany), were very popular in England, their wedding on St. Valentine's Day, 1613, was an occasion for great revelry.

On February 15, the evening after the wedding, the gentlemen of the Middle Temple and Lincoln's Inn pre-

[12] This description of the Middle Temple Christmas celebration of 1599–1600 should not be confused with Davenant's masque by the same name.

[13] Steele considers this masque under "1597–8?" which is nearly as unsatisfactory as 1599–1600. The matter of dating this entertainment has been discussed under the Christmas celebration of 1599.

[14] *Le Prince d'Amour*, pp. 85–90; see also quotation by Steele under date "1597–8?" from J. A. Manning, *Memoirs of Sir Benjamin Rudyerd,* p. 14.

[15] Elizabeth was later known as the Winter Queen of Bohemia.

sented a masque, composed by George Chapman,[16] for the entertainment of the king and the bride and groom. Settings and designs for this *Masque of the Middle Temple and Lincoln's Inn* were fashioned, as the title-page of the edition by George Norton indicates, by "our Kingdomes most Artfull and Ingenious Architect Innigo Jones." The masque is dedicated to Sir Edward Philips, who assisted in the production. This is said to be "A show at all parts so novel, conceitful, and glorious as hath not in this land . . . been ever before beheld."[17] The procession to Whitehall, where the masque was presented, has, however, considerably more merit than the masque itself.

From the residence of Philips, fifty mounted gentlemen, each attended by footmen, set forth, followed by a parade of boys, masked as baboons, on asses. The baboons were illuminated by torches as ridiculously as the gentlemen were gallantly.[18] They were followed by two "cars triumphal," made ornate with mask heads[19] and incrustations of gold and silver. In the cars were twelve musicians, in the habits of Virginian priests; on their heads were turbans, adorned with varicolored feathers, "spotted with wings of flies, of extraordinary bigness, like those of their country."[20] Then came the principal masquers, arrayed in Indian habits, decorated with golden suns and ostrich feathers; their horses were, also, embellished with jewels and suns, and were attended by Moors, in the dress of Indian slaves, and torchbearers.

[16] The similarity between the masque and the play is explained, to some extent, by the fact that both were written by the same person. (Consider, for example, Beaumont and Shirley.) Chapman was later made a member of the Middle Temple Society.

[17] Nichols, *James*, II, 562, *et seq.*

[18] This sort of foil was indispensable to the masque. Note particularly *The Triumph of Peace.*

[19] This is, perhaps, a survival of mumming.

[20] Shepherd, p. 342, and Nichols, *James*, II, 565, *et seq.*

In the last chariot, decorated with paintings and a canopy of gold, rode Capriccio,[21] "half French, half Swiss," and Eunomia,[22] the priest of Honor, and Phemis, her herald. In the most exalted position rode Plutus, or Riches. The royal family and many nobles reviewed the procession from the tiltyard, where the masquers, after making a complete circle the better to display themselves, dismounted to perform the masque.

The masque, a combination of prose, heroic couplets, and lyrics,[23] opens with the display of a magnificent crag, veined with gold. That such an opening scene, which appears in *The Masque of Proteus,* which probably influenced this masque, in *Ulysses and Circe,*[24] and in numerous others, is entirely conventional is recognized by the opening words of this masque: "*Plu.* Rocks! Nothing but rocks in these masking devices! Is Invention so poor she must needs ever dwell amongst rocks?" The rock suddenly breaks, revealing Capriccio. His first speech is also indicative of the popularity of the Proteus and Ulysses themes: "*Cap.* How hard this world is to a man of wit! He must eat through main rocks for his food, or fast. . . . A man must be a second Proteus, and turn himself into all shapes, like Ulysses, to wind through the straits of this pinching vale of misery." After an antic dance by the baboons, Eunomia appears to Plutus at the Temple gates. A second antimasque of torchbearers dances, and finally Honor, representing Elizabeth, is allied to Plutus, who resolves no more to be avaricious. A series of lyrics, somewhat deficient in innuendo and decidedly inferior to those of Beaumont's masque written for the same occasion, is terminated with the following:

[21] This character is well known in the Italian drama.

[22] Law.

[23] This combination is familiar in the dramas of the time.

[24] This masque, of course, succeeded the one under discussion.

Now Sleep, bind fast the flood of air,
Strike all things dumb and deaf,
And to disturb our nuptial pair[25]
Let stir no aspen leaf.
Send flocks of golden dreams
That all true joys presage,
Bring in thy oily streams
The milk-and-honey age.
Now close the world-round sphere of bliss,
And fill it with a heavenly kiss.

John Chamberlain, in a letter to Sir Dudley Carleton,[26] describes this masque as "the best show that hath ben seen many a day." This opinion is, moreover, expressed by Chapman himself in his description of the triumphal procession.[27] It is thought, however, that its success lay rather in subtle blending of elements which had theretofore been successful in the masque than in dramatic creation. This entertainment is said to have cost not less than £1,086 8*s.* 11*d.*[28]

F. THE MASQUE OF THE INNER-TEMPLE AND GRAY'S INN OR *THE MARRIAGE OF THE THAMES AND THE RHINE*

THE gentlemen of the Inner Temple and Gray's Inn, to observe the marriage of Princess Elizabeth to the Count Palatine, presented a masque, usually called *The Masque of*

[25] These verses should be compared with similar ones in the marital hymn which closes Beaumont's masque.

[26] February 18, 1612, State Papers Dom. Jas., I, 72, No. 30; quoted by Nichols, *James*, II, 566–584. Birch, *James*, I, 226, says that this letter was written to Mrs. Carleton.

[27] Chapman's description precedes the printing of the masque in Shepherd and in many other places. It is quoted by Nichols, *James*, II, 550, *et seq.*; late writers have sometimes erroneously referred to it as Nichols' description. Chapman's description attacks Thomas Campion, who produced *The Lord's Masque* on the day preceding.

[28] £50 was borrowed by the Middle Temple from Edward Powell, and £215 from Sir Thomas Temple to defray expenses of this masque (Hopwood, I, 40–41, Parliament, June 18, 1613).

the Inner-Temple and Gray's Inn or *The Marriage of the Thames and the Rhine*, devised by Francis Beaumont,[29] in the Banqueting House at Whitehall on February 20, 1613. That Francis Bacon assisted in the production of this masque is evident from the following dedication to "the worthy Sir Francis Bacon, his Majesty's Solicitor-General":

> Ye that spared no time nor travail in the setting forth, ordering and furnishing of this Masque (being the first fruits of honour in this kind which these two Societies have offered to his majesty) will not think much now to look back upon the effects of your own care and work; for that, whereof the success was then doubtful, is now happily performed and graciously accepted; and that which you were then to think of in straits of time, you may now peruse at leisure: and you, Sir Francis Bacon, especially, as you did then by your countenance and loving affection advance it, so let your good word grace it and defend it, which is able to add value to the greatest and least matters.

Plans were made for the presentation of this masque on Tuesday, February 16, 1613, the night following the entertainment by the gentlemen of the Middle Temple and Lincoln's Inn. As the latter had journeyed to Whitehall on horseback, the gentlemen of the Inner Temple and Gray's, for variety and because the Thames was to be one of the principal actors in their masque, resolved upon a spectacular procession by water. Accordingly, on Tuesday, they embarked in numerous barges and galleys, richly decorated and illuminated, preceded by two admirals. Three salutes of ordnance were given: one at embarkation, one as the fleet passed the Temple garden, and one at debarkation at Whitehall. During the entire voyage, music was played. The transportation by water is said to have cost three hundred pounds. The king, who was much pleased with the display, together with his family, reviewed the procession from the windows

[29] Beaumont was a member of the Inner Temple; his father was justice of the common pleas and, at one time, a bencher of the Inner Temple.

of the privy gallery.[30] Unfortunately, however, as John Chamberlain wrote to Sir Dudley Carleton on February 18,[31]

> they came home as they went without doing anything; the reason whereof I cannot yet learn thoroughly, but only that the Hall was so full that it was not possible to avoid it, or make room for them; besides that most of the Ladies were in the Galleries to see them land, and could not get in. But the worst of all was, that the King was so wearied and sleepy with sitting up almost two whole nights before, that he had no edge to it. Whereupon Sir Francis Bacon ventured to entreat his Majesty, that by this disgrace he would not as it were bury them quick; and I hear the King should answer, that they must bury him quick, for he could last no longer; but withal gave them very good words, and appointed them to come again on Saturday. But the grace of the masque is quite gone, when their apparel hath been already showed, and their devices vented, so that how it will fall out God knows, and the world says it comes to pass after the old proverb, the properer man the worse luck.
>
> One thing I had almost forgotten, that all this time there was a course taken, and so notified, that no lady or gentleman should be admitted to any of these sights with a vardingale, which was to gain more room, and I hope may serve to make them quite left off in time. And yet there were more scaffolds, and more provisions made for room than ever I saw, both in the hall and banqueting room, besides a new room built to dine and dance in.

On the Saturday appointed, the gentlemen were met with special ceremony, and performed their masque with great *éclat*. It opens with dialogue of Mercury and Iris, representatives of Jupiter and Juno, who wish to pay tribute to the wedding of the Thames and the Rhine. This appropriate conception comes originally from Greek mythology, where the wedding of Tethys and Oceanus is well known. Beaumont's idea, however, was probably taken from Spenser's *Faerie Queene* (IV, xi), in which the Thames and the Med-

[30] Birch, *James*, I, 226; Nichols, *James*, II, 588; and Inderwick, Introduction, II, xl, contain good descriptions of this progress.

[31] Quoted by Birch, *James*, I, 226, and elsewhere.

way are married. The first antimasque of Mercury consists of dancing by four Naiads, in sea-green taffeta, who rise from four fountains, and five Hyades, in sky-colored taffeta, who descend from a cloud, symbolizing the fact that rivers are fed by springs and showers, and with them four Cupids, "like naked boys," but inconsistently attired in flame-colored taffeta, and four Statuas,[32] encased with gold and silver. Iris, thinking this show ornate, commands Flora, her companion, to bring in a rural dance. Accordingly, the second antimasque[33] enters, composed of Pedant; May-Lord, May-Lady; Servingman, Chambermaid; Country Clown or Shepherd, Country Wench; Host, Hostess; He-Baboon, She-Baboon; and He-Fool and She-Fool.[34] These antimasques are succeeded by the main masque, in which Mercury, now reconciled with Iris, with her consent brings from two golden pavilions fifteen Olympian knights, who are clad in carnation satin, embroidered with stars of silver. The knights are attended by twelve priests, each playing a lute. Jupiter, through Mercury, thus revives the famous Olympian games. After formal dances by the knights, the gentlemen and ladies dance "galliards, durets, corantos, etc." The priests then sing the concluding song:

> Peace and silence be the guide
> To the man, and to the bride!
> If there be a joy yet new
> In marriage, let it fall on you,
>   That all the world may wonder!
> If we should stay, we should do worse,
> And turn our blessing to a curse,
>   By keeping you asunder.

[32] Statues.

[33] His Majesty asked that the first and second antimasques be repeated, but, as one of the Statuas was then undressed, his wish could not with propriety be gratified.

[34] Most of these figures had, by this time, become stock characters. The second antimasque is usually a foil to the first; the presentation of two characters of the same class but of different sex is common in the masque.

The masque was such a great success that the king invited forty of the masquers and their assistants to a supper in the new "marriage-room, where they were well treated and much graced with kissing his Majesty's hand and every one having a particular *accoglienza* from him."[35] Sir Edward Phelips wrote to Carleton on February 25 that "never Kinge was more gloriously and royally served by them, nor they more honoured or graced by a souvraigne."[36]

The expense of this masque, which cost more than £1,200, apparently above what was allowed by the two houses, was liquidated by special assessments.[37] Besides a levy of £2 10*s*. upon ancients, £2 upon barristers, and 20*s*. upon students at Gray's Inn,[38] order was adopted that the gentlemen should "bring in masking suits whereby some profitt might be made of them."[39]

While *The Masque of the Inner-Temple and Gray's Inn* is not conspicuous among masques, it is graced by delicate lyrics, propriety of costume, and continuity of theme, which make it one of the attractive masques produced by the Inns.

G. THE MASQUE OF FLOWERS

ON January 6 (Twelfth Night), 1614, *The Masque of Flowers* was presented by the gentlemen of Gray's Inn, before James I, in the Banqueting House at Whitehall, in celebration of the marriage of Robert Carr, Earl of Somerset, with the divorced wife of the Earl of Essex.[40] Campion's masque, which was written for presentation on the wedding day, December 26, 1613, is often confused with this masque, and as a consequence it is often said that Campion is the

[35] Birch, I, 229, *James;* see also Nichols, II, 551–552.

[36] State Papers Dom. LXXII, No. 46; quoted by Williamson, pp. 270–273.

[37] Inderwick, II, 72–99, Parliament of May 4, 1613.

[38] Dugdale, p. 286; Douthwaite, p. 230.

[39] Fletcher, I, 206–207.

[40] Ben Jonson wrote *Hymenaei* to celebrate the first marriage of the Countess of Essex, eight years before.

author of *The Masque of Flowers*. The authors, however, are probably the three gentlemen whose initials, "J. G.," "W. D.," and "T. B.," appear at the end of the dedication "To the Very Honourable Knight, Sir Francis Bacon, His Majesty's Attorney-General," in which it is said that Bacon was "the only person that did both encourage and warrant the gentlemen to shew their good affection towards so noble a conjunction in a time of such magnificence."

The masque opens with a dialogue between Invierno,[41] an old man covered with frost and snow and icicles, and Primavera,[42] nude to the waist, but bedecked otherwise with cloth of gold and many flowers. These seasons are commanded by the Sun to present entertainment in honor of the bridal couple. The first antimasque[43] is composed of combat by song and dance between Silenus, friend of Bacchus, and Kawasha[44] as to the merits of wine and tobacco. Silenus, a fat, old man with a red, swollen face, is mounted upon an ass; Kawasha, upon a cowlstaff, is carried by two Indians, attired like Floridians. Each is preceded by a sergeant, four singers, and five musicians. The antimasque of song[45] opens with the following strophe and antistrophe:

Silenus: Ahey for and a ho,
Let's make this great Potan[46]
Drink off Silenus' can;
And when that he well drunk is,
Return him to his munkies
From whence he came.

[41] Winter.

[42] Spring. The influence of the Romanic drama upon this masque is evident throughout.

[43] Called "Antick-Masque."

[44] Evans, p. 102, n.: "In De Bry's collection of voyages (*America*, Part I, Frankfort, 1590) we are informed that the inhabitants of Virginia had an idol called KIWASA."

[45] James I asked that the antimasques of song and dance be repeated for his amusement.

[46] Perhaps Potentate.

Kawasha: Ahey for and a ho,
We'll make Silen fall down
And cast him in a sowne,
To see my men of ire,
All snuffing, puffing, smoke, and fire,
Like fell dragon.

The second antimasque was danced by Pantaloon,[47] Courtezan, Swiss and his Wife; Usurer, Midwife,[48] and Smug and his Wench, representing Silenus; and by Fretelyne,[49] Bawd, Roaring Boy, Citizen, Mountebank, Jewess of Portugal, and Chimney Sweeper and his Wench,[50] representing Kawasha.

With the drawing of a traverse, a beautiful garden is revealed, in which stands a golden Neptune with water flowing from his mouth. As a reversal of the Narcissus story, various flowers in the garden are metamorphosed into men, as are the beasts restored to men in *Ulysses and Circe*. These young gentlemen, thirteen in number, are dressed in white satin doublets, cut in the shape of lilies; their caps are adorned with silk and silver flowers and plumes and egrets. Then, somewhat informally, they dance "corantos, durettos, moriscos," and galliards with the ladies.

The masque closes with the following tribute to the married couple:

Lovely couple, Seasons two
Have performed what they can do;
If the gods inspire our song,
The other two will not stay long.
Receive our Flowers with gracious hand,
As a small wreath to your garland;

[47] A stock character in the Italian drama.
[48] The *accoucheuse* is a figure common in the French drama.
[49] Perhaps a frisker or dancer.
[50] It is interesting to note that many of these characters had, by this time, become well known in the English play.

Flowers of honour, Flowers of beauty
Are your own; we only bring
Flowers of affection, Flowers of duty.

The masquers, after kissing the hands of the king, queen, and prince, were entertained at banquet.

In December, 1613, John Chamberlain wrote to Sir Dudley Carleton, as follows:

> Sir Francis Bacon prepares a Mask to honour this marriage [the marriage of the Lord Rochester] with the divorced Countess of Essex, which will stand him above £2,000; although he have been offered some help by the House,[51] and specially by Mr. Solicitor, Sir Henry Yelverton, who would have sent him £500, he would not accept it, but offers them the whole charge with the honour. Marry, his obligations are such, as well to his Majesty as to the great Lord, and to the whole House of Howards, as he can admit no partners.[52]

The Masque of Flowers was reproduced at Gray's Inn on July 7, 1887, in celebration of the fiftieth anniversary of the coronation of Queen Victoria.[53]

H. THE INNER TEMPLE MASQUE OR *ULYSSES AND CIRCE*

ONE of the most graceful of the Temple masques is that called *The Inner Temple Masque*, or *Ulysses and Circe*, presented, on January 13, 1614–15,[54] in the Inner Temple hall. The author, William Browne, who long resided at the Inner Temple and who dated his *Britannia's Pastorals* from

[51] Gray's Inn.

[52] Quoted by Birch, *James*, II, 282, and by Nichols, *James*, I, 705.

[53] Bacon says in Essay XXXVII, *Of Masques and Triumphs:* "These things are but toys, to come amongst such serious observations. But yet, since princes will have such things, it is better they should be graced with elegancy than daubed with cost." *The Masque of Flowers* is both "graced with elegancy" and "daubed with cost."

[54] Dates herein are made to conform to our present method of computation; this date is, hence, January 13, 1615.

Sir Francis Bacon

that house on June 18, 1613, prefaced this masque with the following modest dedication:

To the Honourable SOCIETY of the
INNER TEMPLE
GENTLEMEN,

I Give you but your owne: If you refuſe to foſter it I knowe not who will: By your meanes it may live. If it degenerate in kinde from thoſe other the ſociety hath produced, blame yourſelves for not ſeeking a happier muſe. I knowe it is not without faultes, yet ſuch as your loves, or at leaſt Poetica Licentia (the common ſalve) will make tollerable: What is good in it, that is yours; what bad, myne; what indifferent, both; and that will ſuffice, ſince it was done to pleaſe ourſelves in private, by him that is

All yours,
W. BROWNE.

This masque, having been written "to pleaſe ourſelves in private," is, unlike the ordinary masque, entirely independent of occasion.

Ulysses and Circe, which has a unity extraordinary in the masque, is based upon the classical story found in the tenth book of the *Odyssey*, in which the companions of Ulysses are transformed into beasts through the sorcery of Circe and are reclaimed by Ulysses. In every case, Browne cites the source of his inspiration, which includes Homer, Hyginus, Servius, Apollonius, Virgil, and Ovid. This masque, however, is, in no sense, a rehash; it reveals everywhere the light and skilful touch of original genius. One may well wish that Browne had written other masques.

The principal dialogists are Ulysses, Circe, Syren, and Triton. Wood nymphs, satyrs, and a woodman are among the minor characters.

This masque, which is much like *The Masque of Proteus*, is divided into three scenes. It also opens with a sea cliff as a setting; upon the cliff, which is on the Aeaean Island, the sea being in perspective, are seated two sirens, who are described, with a curious blending of the classical and the homely, as having "their upper parts like women to the navell, and the reſt like a hen."

The masque begins with a song by one of the sirens, as in the opening of *The Masque of Proteus*. Part of the song is repeated "as from a grove nere" by a chorus, another importation from the Greek drama.

At the beginning of the second scene, when Circe says, "Yond ſtandes a hill," a "travers was drawne," discovering a wood, upon the hillocks of which are seated eight musicians, probably those retained permanently by the Inn. A footnote says that "The muſicke was composed of treble violins, with all the inward parts, a baſe violle, baſe lute, ſagbut, cornamute, and a tabor and pipe."

During the singing, the scene is changed several times, usually by simply drawing a curtain.

Unlike *The Masque of Proteus*, this masque contains two antimasques, the first comprised of the beasts into which Circe has transformed the knights: two of them are stags, like Actaeon; two have asses' ears, like Midas; two are wolves, like Lycaon; two are baboons; and one is Grillus, a "hogge." It was only his close friendship with the gentlemen of the Inn that permitted Browne this liberty of transforming them so. The first antimasque indicates the dramatic possibilities of the story of Ulysses, which were very evident to Browne, who developed them fully. The woodman sings, then, the following song about Grillus:

GRILLUS is gone, belyke he hath hearde
The dayrie-maid knocke at the trough in the yearde:
  Through thicke and thinne he wallowes,
  And weighes nor depths nor ſhallowes.
Hark! how he whynes,
Run all e're he dines,
  Then ſerve him a tricke
  For beinge ſo quicke,

And lette him for all his paines
Behold you turne cleane of
His troughe,
And ſpill all his waſh and his graines.

Echo is then introduced from Greek literature, and joins in the following song with the woodman:

CIRCE bids you come awaye.
ECCHO. Come awaye, come awaye.
From the rivers, from the ſea.
ECCHO. From the ſea, from the ſea.
From the greene woods every one.
ECCHO. Every one, every one.
Of her maides be miſſinge none.
ECCHO. Miſſinge none, miſſinge none.
No longer ſtay, except it be to bringe
A med'cine for love's ſtinge.
That would excuſe you, and be held more deare,
Than wit or magicke, for both they are here.
ECCHO. They are here, they are here.

This song presents the second antimasque, composed of seven nymphs, four in white, with chaplets of flowers, and three in "ſea greene robes, greeniſh haire hanging looſe, with leaves of corall and ſhells intermixt upon it."[55]

After dancing by the nymphs, the third scene is presented. Ulysses, much like Proteus, touches with his wand several trees, whereupon a pleasing walk is discovered, with the rising sun at the end. The knights of Ulysses, restored to human form, are, at the same time, disclosed. Their costume, it will be seen, is appropriately artistic:

Doublets of greene taffita, cut like oaken leaves, as upon cloth of ſylver; their ſkirtes and winges cut into leaves, deepe round hoſe

[55] Bacon (*Of Maſques and Triumphs*) says that the following are the chief requisites of the masque: "choirs must be placed near over against another; colours of White, carnation, and a kind of sea-water green,—graceful suits . . . sweet odours suddenly coming forth."

of the ſame, both lin'd with ſprigge lace ſpangled; long white ſylke ſtockings; greene pumps, and roſes done over with ſylver leaves; hattes of the ſame ſtuffe, and cut narrowe-brimmed, and riſinge ſmaller compaſſe at the crowne; white reathe hatbandes; white plumes; egrettes with a greene fall; ruffe bands and cuffes.

After dancing galliards, courantes, and brawls with their ladies, Time calls the knights away. The rising of the sun, after the gaiety had continued all night, became, during the early seventeenth century, a conventional method of terminating the masque. *Ulysses and Circe* closes with the following graceful song:

WHO but Time ſo haſty were,
To fly away and leave you here.
Here where delight
Might well allure
A very ſtoicke, from this night
To turne an epicure.

But ſince he calles away; and time will ſoone repent,
He ſtaid not longer here, but ran to be more idly ſpente.[56]

This masque, one of the most poetic in the language, was so popular that guests climbed on the outer window sills to get glimpses of the entertainment. In their eagerness, the throng destroyed the chimney of George Lowe, the chief cook, who, in consequence, petitioned the society for indemnity.[57]

Ulysses and Circe has so many attributes in common with *Comus* that it seems to have inspired Milton.[58] Its influence

[56] This song is, in some editions, followed by the words, "Τέλος," "Finis," and "End," showing not only that Browne knew the classics, but indisputably that the play is over.

[57] Inderwick, II, xlii and 95.

[58] *Comus* is not a true masque, because there are no formal dances and no company of masquers; moreover, the music is subordinate; moreover, the principals, because of their identification with the Earl of Bridgewater, do not attain complete allegorical or mythological character (Evans, p. xxxiii, n.).

upon other masques of the seventeenth century was unquestionably considerable.

I. THE MASQUE OF MOUNTEBANKS

ON February 2, 1618, the gentlemen of Gray's Inn produced in their hall *The Masque of Mountebanks;*[59] it was presented at court on February 16, 1618. John Payne Collier, who, in 1848, printed this entertainment for the Shakespeare Society from a manuscript in the possession of the Duke of Devonshire, asserted it to be the composition of John Marston, principally because Marston's name appears in pencil on the manuscript. When one recalls similar notations on the Shakespeare second folio, one cannot accept unqualifiedly the statement of Collier. The version presented at court was printed by Nichols[60] before Collier published the Duke of Devonshire's manuscript, which contains numerous paradoxes omitted by the former. It is now generally believed that this masque originally formed a part of the *Gesta Grayorum* for Christmas, 1617–18.[61]

This masque is quite distinctive, in that it is no more than a satire of the methods of the mountebank, and it may be a double satire in that it appears to be a burlesque imitation of the type of masque introduced by the mountebanks who had begun to rent theaters during the Lenten season.[62] Moreover, it had long been the custom to satirize the mountebank in the French theater, where recipes and almanacs were distributed to the audience.[63]

A letter from John Chamberlain to Sir Dudley Carleton[64] describes the entertainment:

[59] This entertainment is called also *The Mountebank's Masque.*

[60] *Progresses of James,* III, 468.

[61] Fleay, *B. C.,* II, 82.

[62] Lawrence, p. 331.

[63] Welsford, pp. 203–204. See recipes from the French in Davenant's *Salmacida Spolia.*

[64] Nichols, *James,* III, 468, and Steele, pp. 201–202.

On Thursday night the gentlemen of Gray's Inn came to the court with their show, for I cannot call it a masque, seeing they were not disguised, nor had vizards. For the rest, their fashion and device were well approved, though it were thought to be somewhat out of season to revel in Lent.

The masque opens with a speech, in the nature of an anti-masque, by the principal mountebank, in which Aesculapius and Paracelsus are paid tribute. A Greek chorus then sings of the curative powers of the mountebanks, declaring that none shall be "vex'd with kibes or corns" or cuckolds with their horns. This is followed by a number of amusing "familiar receipts," the first of which follows:

An approved receipt against Melancholy feminine.

If any Lady be sick of the Sullens, she knows not where, let her take a handful of simples, I know not what, and use them I know not how, applying them to the part grieved, I know not which, and she shall be well, I know not when.

Then Paradox, "a slip of darkness," whose mother is an Anabaptist and whose father a Jesuit, enters and propounds various masculine, feminine, and neuter paradoxes, some of which follow:

A Drunkard is a good philosopher; for he thinks aright that the world goes round.

Downright language is the best Rhetoric to win a woman; for plain dealing is a jewel, and there is no lady but desires her lap full of them.

Old things are the best things; for there is nothing new but diseases.

The best bodies should wear the plainest habits; for painted Clothes were made to hide bare walls.

Playhouses are more necessary in a well governed Commonwealth than public Schools; for men are better taught by example than precept.

Taverns are more requisite in a City than Academies; for it is better the multitude were loving than learned.

The Court makes better Scholars than the University; for where a King vouchsafes to be a teacher, every man blushes to be a non-proficient.

The more extravagant of these three-hundred-year-old paradoxes make one question the sophistication of our own age. The main masque then begins with the appearance of four pages and Obscurity. The following song, which has made this masque rather well known, is then sung:

Frolic measures now become you,
Overlong obscured Knights:
What if Lethe did benumb you,
Love now wakes you to delights.
Love is like a golden flower,
Your comely youth adorning:
Pleasure is a gentle shower
Shed in some April morning.

Lightly rise, and lightly fall you
In the motion of your feet:
Move not till our notes do call you;
Music makes the action sweet.
Music breathing blows the fire
Which Cupid feeds with fuel,
Kindling honour and desire,
And taming hearts most cruel.

Music is the soul of measure,
Mixing both in equal grace;
Twins are they, begot of Pleasure,
When she wisely numbered space.
Nothing is more old or newer
Then number, all advancing;
And no number can be truer
Than music joined with dancing.

Every Knight elect a Beauty,
Such as may thy heart inflame:
Think that her bright eye doth view thee,
And to her thy action frame.
So shall none be faint or weary,
Though treading endless paces;
For they all are light and merry
Whose hopes are fed with graces.

Sprightly, sprightly, end your paces,
Nimbly changing measured graces:
Lively mounted high aspire,
For joy is only found in fire.

After dancing with the ladies, Paradox returns with his disciples, who dance an antimasque. Then, in accordance with the conventional satire of the French and the Swiss, Mountebank enters, attired like a Swiss. After dialogue between the principal characters, the night of revel is ended traditionally with the banishment of Night and the appearance of Day.

The Masque of Mountebanks is interesting not in mythological or allegorical conception or in scenic display, but in the fact that its motif is burlesque; in this respect, it is unique among the masques presented by the Inns.

From the correspondents of Sir Dudley Carleton, who was then the English ambassador at The Hague, we learn that this masque was presented at court on the first Thursday in Lent: Nathanael Brent[65] says that the masque "pleased tolerably well," that the eighteen masquers danced gracefully, and that the "wittie ribalderie . . . made the companie merrie." Sir Gerrard Herbert,[66] in speaking of the same performance, says that the music was good, that the dancing, some of which was done to the voices of boys, was well per-

[65] State Papers Dom., Jas. I, xcvi, 24; quoted by Douthwaite, p. 230. (Letter dated February 21, 1617 [1618].)

[66] State Papers, Dom., Jas. I, xcvi, 27, quoted by Douthwaite, p. 230. (Letter dated February 22, 1618.)

formed, and that the part of Paradox was executed so well that the actor was highly commended. The gentlemen of Gray's, having kissed the king's hand, were led to a splendid banquet, where his Majesty "wild them to fall to it."

J. THE INNER-TEMPLE MASQUE OR *THE MASQUE OF HEROES*

AT Christmas, 1618–19, the gentlemen of the Inner Temple produced *The Inner-Temple Masque*, or *The Masque of Heroes*, one of the most native and sportive of the masques presented at the Inns. The sheer joviality of this masque prevents it from being repulsively lascivious.[67] Ironically enough, this entertainment was presented for the diversion of "many worthy Ladies."[68] Middleton asserts originality for his composition in the following flyleaf inscription:

> This nothing owes to any tale or story
> With which some writer pieces up a glory;
> I only made the time, they sat to see,
> Serve for the mirth itself, which was found free;
> And herein fortunate, that's counted good,
> Being made for ladies, ladies understood.
>
> T. M.

Although the original vivacity of this masque may not be depreciated, the conception of representing symbolically the holiday observed by the masque is, in no sense, a departure.

The edition printed for John Browne in 1619 contains the following list of characters:

THE PARTS.	THE SPEAKERS.
Doctor Almanac	JOS. TAYLOR.[69]

[67] Many critics have unqualifiedly condemned this masque as being coarse, an objection which may not be definitely refuted. The Rev. Mr. Alexander Dyce, an editor of Middleton, seems, however, not to have been offended.

[68] From title of Browne edition of 1619.

[69] Taylor and the other four named actors were at this time with the Alleyn company at the Fortune Theatre.

Plumporridge	W. ROWLEY.
A Fasting-Day	J. NEWTON.
New Year	H. ATWELL.
Time	W. CARPENTER.
Harmony	*A Boy.*

The masque opens with dialogue between Doctor Almanac, who is returning from the funeral of Old Year, and Fasting-Day, who is recognizable by his gauntness and thin chitterlings. Fasting-Day laments that he has been

> . . . out of service all this
> Kersmas; . . . [70]
> Nobody minds Fasting-Day;
> I've scarce been thought upon a' Friday nights;
> . . . the butchers' boys
> At Temple-Bar set their great dogs upon me.

Plumporridge then enters, and calls Fasting-Day "a lean, spiny rascal, with a dog in's belly; his very bowels bark with hunger." Doctor Almanac then says that he saw Kersmas "very lusty a' Twelfth Night." Thus, the customs of keeping fast days and of anticipating the time for observing Christmas are satirized, like many other customs at the Inns. All restraining influences, particularly the Puritans and the Anabaptists, are severely ridiculed. The will of Kersmas, who had not much to bequeath, because "his children have so consumed him beforehand," is read. The terminology of the will, which is drawn in entirely correct legal form, would be in decidedly bad taste if it were not known that most of the names which seem offensive are those of card games. This masque is somewhat different, in that it deals with the entertainments and studies of the gentlemen of the Inner Temple. After two attractive antimasques, the first composed of Candlemas-day, Shrove-Tuesday, Lent, Ill May-Day, Midsummer-Eve, and The First Dog-Day, and the

[70] Christmas.

second of Three Good Days, Three Bad Days, and Two Indifferent Days, Harmony is discovered, and sings rather graceful seasonal songs. Then Time enters and terminates the masque by saying,

> The morning gray,
> Bids come away.

This ending, which is thoroughly conventional, appears in *The Triumph of Peace* and in numerous other masques.

The Masque of Heroes, which takes its name from the fact that the gentlemen of the Inner Temple are discovered as "deified heroes sitting in arches of clouds,"[71] just before their dance with the ladies, is important in that it adopts purely English atmosphere and humor, rejecting altogether the characters of Greek mythology which had theretofore been popular in the masque, and in that it is the true product of the Inner Temple, being based upon the traditions, customs, and restrictions of that house.

K. THE TRIUMPH OF PEACE

THE most spectacular masque presented by the Inns of Court, and perhaps the most luxurious ever produced in England, is *The Triumph of Peace*, by James Shirley,[72] devised as a token of affection for the sovereign, and, also, to liberate both the Inns and the royal court from the tentacles of the Puritans.

In 1633, William Prynne, an utter barrister of Lincoln's Inn, made hell's foundations quiver with his *Histriomastix*, an attack upon plays, "the very Pompes of the Divell,"—a burning assertion having some semblance of truth. Prynne the Puritan, having felt the hot breath of the unholy ghost,

[71] Inderwick, II, xlv.

[72] The introduction of the realistic comic element into this masque may, perhaps, be attributed to the fact that Shirley was also a composer of the popular drama. Shirley, at this time, resided at Gray's Inn.

became so much enraged that he said that women actors and notorious whores have some attributes in common. Unfortunately, however, Prynne did not confine his statement to professionals. More unfortunately, six weeks after this time, the queen played in a pastoral at Somerset House. A short while afterward, Archbishop Laud and other praiseworthy gentlemen presented the king with a copy of *Histriomastix*, with the information that the section on women actors was prepared as an attack upon the queen. In reality, the book was written considerably before the queen's indiscretion.[73] Prynne, instead of vanquishing the fiery demon, had most of the copies of his book burned, rather incongruously but in accordance with usual practice, by the common hangman; moreover, he was shorn of his Midas-ears, and was fined £5,000 and imprisoned for life, besides being disbarred and expelled from Lincoln's Inn.[74]

Naturally, the court was embarrassed, as were the Inns, one of whose members had offended the crown. The situation was aggravated by the fact that many of the common people were in sympathy with Prynne. Lincoln's Inn then appropriately suggested to the court that a masque, as a visible sign of a spiritual friendship, be presented before the royal house.[75] Bulstrode Whitelock, who was in charge of the music of the masque, says that the hint was given at court, where it was considered that such a demonstration would be welcome and particularly seasonable because of the recent attack by Prynne.[76] Whitelock's biographer,[77] writing two centuries later, says, however, that the suggestion came originally from the court, whereupon the "obsequious

[73] Whitelock's *Memorials*, I, 51–52.

[74] *Ibid.*, pp. 62–63. ("Whitelock" is the approved spelling of this name; the biographer, however, spells his name "Whitelocke.")

[75] Herbert, p. 313.

[76] Whitelock's *Memorials*, I, 53.

[77] R. H. Whitelocke, *Memoirs of Bulstrode Whitelocke*, p. 94.

Societies, . . . entirely dependent on court favour and money for advancement to place and honours," decided to present the masque. Contemporary evidence,[78] however, indicates that the plan was initially that of the gentlemen of the Inns, and that the masque was produced not only because of the attack of Prynne, but also because it had long been the custom for the gentlemen to entertain the sovereign in this manner as a mark of friendship, and, further, because of the recent birth of the Duke of York. The Bench Minute Books of the Middle Temple indicate, under date of October 25, 1633, a levy made upon each of the members of that house toward a fund of £600 to be contributed by each of the four Inns for entertainment in observance of the birth of the king's second son. The following record[79] of the Inner Temple indicates likewise an assessment for the production of this masque:

> Whereas there having been no representation of any mask or other show before the King's Majesty by the four Inns of Court or any of them sithens his Highness' access unto the Crown, a consultation hath been lately had by the several benchers in their several Houses touching the same, whereupon it is unanimously agreed by them that a mask shall be jointly presented in this next Christmas before his Majesty, at the equall charges of the said four Houses. . . . every fellow of this House shall be taxed to pay as followeth, viz.: Every bencher, 5li.; every utter barrister of seven years' standing 50s.; every utter barrister under seven years' standing, 40s.; every gentleman under the bar . . . 20s.

Approximately £890 was collected at the Inner Temple alone.[80] It will be seen, thus, that the entire cost of this masque was more than £24,000, although the sum quoted

[78] Notwithstanding letter of Thomas Coke of October 17, which says that the request came from the king (MSS of Earl Cowper, Hist. MSS Com., Ap. to Twelfth Report, 2, p. 34).

[79] Inderwick, II, 210, Parliament, November 12, 1633.

[80] *Ibid.*, xlvi.

by various authorities varies from £20,000 to £24,000. This amount is probably the equivalent of a million dollars in money of the United States at the present time.

A committee of two was chosen from each house to make plans for the masque, which was to be presented on Candlemas night (February 2), 1634. The Middle Temple was represented by Edward Hyde, afterward Lord Chancellor Clarendon, and Bulstrode Whitelock,[81] afterward lord keeper[82] and ambassador to Sweden; the Inner Temple by Sir Edward Herbert and John Selden; Lincoln's Inn by Mr. Attorney-General Noy, of ship money fame, and Mr. Gerling; Gray's Inn by Sir John Finch, who became attorney-general, chief justice of common pleas, and lord keeper of the great seal, and by a gentleman who cannot now be identified.

Scenery and ornamentation for *The Triumph of Peace* were prepared by Inigo Jones, surveyor of the king's works, who likewise designed the settings for *The Masque of the Middle Temple and Lincoln's Inn.*

The chairman of the sub-committee on music was Bulstrode Whitelock,[83] who appointed Simon Ives[84] and William Lawes[85] to compose the airs. Bulstrode, moreover, retained the distinguished French musicians[86] of the queen's chapel, as well as English, Scotch,[87] Italian, and German musicians;

[81] Whitelock (*Memorials,* I, 51–63), has left a minute description of this masque.

[82] Four of these eight gentlemen later became keepers of the great seal.

[83] The biographer of Whitelock (R. H. Whitelocke) says that his mind "seems to have become unhinged," with the result that he turned from Coke, Little, and Bracton to lutists and harpers, and, with the assistance of Ives, composed an air, called "Whitelocke's Coranto," which was played whenever he went to the theater.

[84] Whitelock calls him "Simon Ivy."

[85] William Lawes, it will be recalled, assisted his brother, Henry, in the composition of the music for *The Prince d'Amour.*

[86] Messieurs la Mare, du Vall, Robert, and Mari.

[87] R. H. Whitelocke (*Memoirs,* p. 95) speaks of "Hideous bagpipes, squeaking hornpipes, and other kinds of 'northern music.' "

thus, the music of each of the prominent nations was represented. Forty lutes and many other instruments were played at one time. In fact, the music was so ravishing that Whitelock himself had to say that "it excelled any music that ever before that time had been heard in England."[88] Ives and Lawes were given a hundred pounds each for their services, and the French musicians were invited to dinner at St. Dunstan's, where each found forty gold pieces in his napkin.[89] The total cost of the music was a thousand pounds.

On the afternoon of Candlemas day, the gentlemen of the four Inns met at Ely House, in Holborn, and began the magnificent procession down Chancery Lane; thence to Whitehall.[90] The marshal, Mr. Darrel of Lincoln's Inn, and his twenty footmen, clad in scarlet and silver, each carrying a baton and a torch, cleared the streets. Then followed a hundred young gentlemen, each house being represented by its twenty-five most handsome residents, with their rich gold and silver lace sparkling, mounted upon the noblest horses in the kingdom. Three hundred servants attended the gentlemen, a page and two lackeys being assigned to each one. Then came the first antimasque, composed of beggars and cripples, "snapping and yet playing in a consort"[91] upon keys and tongs. They, too, were mounted, but on the leanest and most diseased horses that the knackers could provide. This was followed by various men on horseback playing on pipes and whistles as though they were birds. Then came the antimasque, composed of boys, costumed like owls and various other birds, riding upon ponies. After a procession of musicians playing bagpipes and similar instruments followed the antimasque satirizing the monopolistic patent laws,[92] and particularly the Statute of 21 James I (c.3), considered to be the

[88] Whitelock's *Memorials*, I, 53.
[89] R. H. Whitelocke's *Memoirs*, p. 97.
[90] Whitelock's *Memorials*, I, 54. [91] *Ibid.*, p. 57.
[92] Attorney-General Noy probably prepared this antimasque.

basis of the patent evil. The first in the antimasque of projectors was a man with a horse's bit in his mouth, indicating that all in the kingdom must buy bits of him; the second was a man with carrots on his head and a capon on his wrist, signifying that he was possessed of the monopoly of feeding capons with carrots. Six of the principal musicians, costumed as heathen priests, preceded a handsome chariot, drawn by six horses decorated with plumes; in the chariot were twelve persons clad like gods and goddesses. Three more similar troops of musicians preceded the procession of grand masquers, for whom chariots much like those of the Romans were specially built. According to lot, the gentlemen of Gray's Inn rode in the first chariot, which was decorated in silver and crimson[93] and richly carved by hand, the four delegates being abreast, that question of precedence might not arise. These gentlemen, dressed in doublets covered with silver spangles, were attended by four footmen, lighting the way with flambeaux. In similar manner rode the four representatives of the Middle Temple in a chariot of silver and blue, those of the Inner Temple in one of silver and crimson,[94] and those of Lincoln's Inn in one of silver and white. The royal family reviewed the parade from a window facing the street, and were so well pleased that they sent a request that the participants encircle the tiltyard, that they might obtain another view of them.

The Banqueting House at Whitehall had been decorated for the performance of the masque. Figures of Minos and Numa, great festoons of fruit, and olive branches symbolized Peace, Justice, and Law.

The Triumph of Peace is, perhaps, the most heterogeneous of the masques produced by the Inns. The unifying theme, if there be any, is just what it should have been: Peace, aided

[93] Evans says that the colors of Gray's Inn were silver and orange.

[94] These are the colors given by Evans. There is clearly much confusion in Whitelock's color scheme.

and abetted by Justice and Law, call to pay tribute to the sovereign. Shirley's dedication "to the Four Equal and Honourable Societies, the Inns of Court," celebrates "our Kingdom so blest in the present government." The mere list of characters reveals the conglomerate nature of this masque:

Opinion	Carpenter	Irene
Confidence	Tailor	Eunomia
Fancy	Blackguard	Diche
Jollity	Painter	Genius
Laughter	Tailor's Wife	Amphiluche
Novelty	Property Man's Wife	The Hours
Admiration	Feather Maker's Wife	Chorus
	Embroiderer's Wife	
	Guards	

The first part of the entertainment is devoted to antimasques. As indicative of the popularity of this lower form of diversion, when Fancy is told that there are no antimasques, she says, "No antimasque! Bid 'em down with the scene, and sell the timber." Thereupon an antimasque is improvised: the characters dance in manners expressive of their natures. A second antimasque is then danced by a *maquerelle*,[95] two wenches, and two gamesters, each revealing his nature; cripples, upon whom charity has been bestowed, discard their crutches and join in the dance. Then enter, in turn, six projectors. One has a cooking utensil which can

> Boil beef so thoroughly, that the very steam
> Of the first vessel shall alone be able
> To make another pot above seethe over.

Another has

> A case to walk you all day under water;
> So vast for the necessity of air,
> Which, with an artificial bellows cool'd,

[95] Bawd; a popular figure in the French drama.

Under each arm is kept still from corruption;
With those glass eyes he sees, and can fetch up
Gold or whatever jewels ha' been lost,
In any river o' the world,

and a third has an apparatus that will "Compose a ship to sail against the winds." The interesting thing to us is that all these ideas have been found practicable. This is followed by a dance of the birds; then successively by two thieves robbing a horseman and being captured by a constable; three satyrs attempting to deflower four nymphs, who are rescued by four huntsmen; three dotterels[96] being caught by fowlers; a fantastic knight attempting a windmill,[97] and a country gentleman and his servant being assaulted by the knight; and four bowlers, showing much skill and variety in their sport. Thus the antimasque, quite as illogical and inharmonious as modern vaudeville, is concluded. On a white cloud then appears Irene, or Peace, with a garland of olives on her head; from another cloud, of "orient color," appears Eunomia, or Law, clad in legal purple, adorned with golden stars; and from a third cloud of varied colors appears Diche, or Justice, in a white robe. Each of the goddesses sings a delicate lyric, after which all of them sing the following ode to the king and queen:

To you, great king and queen, whose smile
Doth scatter blessings through this isle,
    To make it best
    And wonder of the rest
We pay the duty of our birth;
Proud to wait upon that earth
    Whereon you move,
    Which shall be nam'd,
And by your chaste embraces fam'd,
    The paradise of love.

[96] Birds that are said to mimic the fowler, thus permitting them to be captured easily.

[97] This is probably taken from *Don Quixote*.

Irene, plant thy olives here;
Thus warm'd, at once they'll bloom and bear;
Eunomia, pay thy light;
While Diche, covetous to stay,
Shall throw her silver wings away,
To dwell within your sight.

Sixteen gentlemen, the sons of Peace, Law, and Justice, then form a pyramidal figure, after which they dance. Everyone is then disturbed by noise, whereupon all the property keepers, the painter, the tailor, and others, enter and demand the right to take part in the dancing. The introduction of these characters of low life into the masque, which is by no means unusual, may have been originated by Ben Jonson. After the revels are over, a faint light breaks over "a plain champaign country," and a beautiful young maiden, Amphiluche, or Dawn, appears,[98] and the masquers are called from their revels.

After the masque, the gentlemen of the Inns were entertained at a luxurious banquet. Sir John Finch, in his most gallant manner, expressed to the king the appreciation of the four Inns for his gracious acceptance of their entertainment, to which both the king and queen responded with affability.[99]

The queen, much pleased with *The Triumph of Peace,* requested its presentation again, whereupon the Lord Mayor of London requested that he be permitted to be host to the royal family and to the four houses at its second production. Moreover, the king invited one hundred and twenty gentlemen of the Inns to a masque in which he was to participate within a short time.[100]

[98] The appearance of Dawn is a convention. It is to be found, for example, in *Ulysses and Circe.*

[99] Whitelock's *Memorials,* p. 62.

[100] Letter of Philip Herbert, Lord Chamberlain, to Thomas, Lord Coventry, quoted in Black Book, II, Appendix XII.

Although *The Triumph of Peace* has continued to hold a relatively high place among English masques, it has, with the exception of the lyrics, little literary merit; its success probably lay in the magnificence of the triumphal procession, in rich costuming, and in grandeur of scenic effects.[101]

L. THE TRIUMPHS OF THE PRINCE D'AMOUR

IN November, 1634, Charles, Prince Palatine of the Rhine, then eighteen years old, came to England for assistance in effecting his restoration to the palatinate. On February 24, 1635, the Middle Temple presented for his entertainment and that of his brother, Rupert, a masque entitled *The Triumphs of the Prince d'Amour.* This masque takes its name from the officer annually elected at the Middle Temple to conduct the Christmas revels.

The Prince d'Amour, as this masque is usually called, is distinctly occasional, but its propriety to the occasion may be impugned without difficulty. It is decidedly ununified and kaleidoscopic. As it is lacking in dialogue, it is little more than dumb show.

This masque opens with an address to the princes by the master of ceremonies, in which the freedom of the Temple is offered to the princes.

At the upper end of the hall was a stage, over which appeared the inscription,

"LES TRIUMPHES DU PRINCE D'AMOUR."

The rise of the curtain discovered a village of alehouses and tobacco shops, in which were exchanging greetings the

[101] The pension of May 12, 1634, at Gray's Inn adopted the following resolution: "The chambers of all gentlemen of the house who do not pay their taxations for the late masque before Thursday next are to be seized to the use of the house" (Fletcher, I, 320). During performance of the masque, the Earl of Pembroke broke his cane over the head of Thomas May of Gray's Inn, translator of Lucan's "Pharsalia." On the next day, Pembroke comforted May with a present of fifty pounds (Bellot, p. 6).

players of the first antimasque, two soldiers, two Dutch sea officers, a gunner and a boatswain, a Cavalier, a begging soldier, and a sutler's wife. A sudden change of scenery reveals the statue of Mars. The priests of Mars, clad in crimson robes, sing the following song:

Come shut our Temple and away,
Our bold seditions God shall stay;
We'll serve no sacrifice to day,
Our humour is to feast, not pray.

The battle which our knights have won,
Did last until th' amazed sun,
For fear, did mend his usual pace,
And set betimes to hide his face.

And now the story of their fight
Is universal, as his light,
Which Fame upon her swifter wing
Hath early brought for us to sing.

After various other songs of battle, the scene suddenly changes, and numerous Knights Templars appear in Roman martial habits, richly embroidered; the beavers of their plumed helmets, falling over their faces, serve as vizards. The defenders of the faith are rapidly supplanted by Cupid, precipitated to the earth in a bright cloud. For variety, and probably not continuing the Cupid motif, the scene changes to a Venetian Piazza, where are many courtezans of numerous countries. Anachorism was not of great import to William Davenant, who composed the masque. Furthermore, five lovers, each of different nationality, a "formal" Spaniard, a "jealous" Italian, a "giddy fantastic" Frenchman, a "dull" Dutchman, and a "furious debauch'd" Englishman, gesticulate madly to the women. While this scene is, strictly speaking, a counterpoint, its fitness as entertainment for the queen and two princes, eighteen and sixteen years old, may be impugned. However, Davenant dismisses the courtezans briefly, and the scene changes first to the Temple of Venus and then to the Temple of Apollo, where, in each place, priests sing. Finally, twelve men, appearing to be naked to the waist, but covered with green fringe to the knees, present themselves. The charger which each bears, filled with luscious fruit, is placed with the others, forming a luxurious banquet. The masque closes with a song of valediction by the priests of Mars, Venus, and Apollo and the entire chorus.

The music for the masque was composed by Mr. Henry and Mr. William Lawes.[102]

The Prince d'Amour, disjointed though it be, contains many conventional masque elements: songs and dancing, tributes to royalty, a chorus, rapid change of scenery through use of a machine, and a very general theme throughout, suggested by the title.

Davenant says in the preface to this masque that it was "devis'd and written in three days," which may account for its very patent imperfections.

The queen, who was one of the guests at this entertainment, put "off majesty to putt on a citizens habitt, and to sett upon the scaffold on the right hande amongst her subjects." Her Majesty said that "she liked it very well"[103] when she left. Attending the queen were the Marchioness Hamilton, the countesses of Denbighe and Holland, and Lady Elizabeth Fielding, all clad in citizens' habits. The Earl of Holland and Lord Goring attended, also. Henry Herbert says that this masque was "very well performed in the dances, scenes, cloathinge, and musique."

[102] It will be recalled that Henry Lawes composed the music for Milton's *Comus*, and his brother William, "the father of musick," as Charles called him, that for Shirley's masque, *The Triumph of Peace*.

[103] Fleay, *B. C.*, p. 319.

M. GRAY'S INN MASQUE OF FEBRUARY 2, 1683

IN the *Diary* of Narcissus Luttrell may be found record of a masque presented at Gray's Inn on Candlemas day (February 2), 1683. Under date of November, 1682, Luttrell says that, on the fourth day of that month, the revels began at Gray's Inn, and, in February, 1683, he says that Sir Richard Gipps,[104] who had been knighted by Charles II on November 27, 1682, visited the court on the twenty-third of January for the purpose of inviting the royal family to attend the Candlemas day masque at Gray's Inn. Gipps, who later was reprimanded for trampling under foot some salutary orders which had been affixed to the screen in the hall, was admitted to Gray's on February 5, 1675, and agreed to be master of the revels, on November 3, 1682. It is interesting that one of the tickets of admission to this performance, bearing the name of Gipps, has been preserved; Nichols, who reproduces it,[105] obtained it from Sir Thomas Gery Cullum, who purchased it from an itinerant peddler. In the records of the Inn may be found entry of an order upon the treasurer to pay the master of the revels for constructing scaffolds for the production of the masque.[106] Luttrell[107] says that many of the nobility appeared in masks at the hall of Gray's Inn, where they were entertained, a banquet following the general dancing. It is probable that this masque was not so spectacular as those of the early seventeenth century, in spite of the fact that, with the Restoration, an attempt was made to restore the grandeur of this form of entertainment, which was being fast displaced by the play. It is probable that this masque was little more than

[104] Sometimes Gibbs. Gipps's entertainment of the nobility with dances is noted in *The Loyal Protestant* of November 14, 1682.

[105] *Elizabeth,* I, xx–xxi, and xxl, n.

[106] Fletcher, II, 69, Pension, November 3, 1682.

[107] February, 1683.

the usual Christmas celebration, marked by foolery, dancing, and singing, followed by a banquet.

N. *MISCELLANEOUS MASQUES*

WHILE no attempt will be made to collate the innumerable references in the records of the Inns of Court to masques, a few of the less important may be noticed. On January 17, 1617, the Middle Temple entertained the Earl of Buckingham with a masque;[108] on February 13, 1621, the same Inn presented a masque before the king, at which the six commissioners from the States of the United Provinces were guests;[109] on January 12, 1628, the Rev. Mr. Joseph Mead wrote to Sir Martin Stuteville that the gentlemen of the Temple were to present a masque at Shrovetide (February 24–26) before the royal family;[110] and late in November, a masque was presented at the Middle Temple, before which the benchers sang the 100th Psalm and drank hipocras.[111, 112]

[108] Fleay, *B. C.*, p. 182.

[109] Nichols, *James*, IV, 653; and *Finetti Philoxenis*, pp. 73–74, and *Cal. State Papers, Venetian*, 1619–21, p. 579, quoted by Steele, 1620–21.

[110] Steele, 1627–28, February 24, quoting Birch, *Court and Times of Charles I*, pp. i, 312.

[111] Gardener's *History of the Commonwealth*, II, 11–12, quoted by Pitt-Lewis, p. 82, and the news sheet *Perfect Passages of Everie Daies Intelligence from the Parliament Army under the Command of His Excellency the Lord General Cromwell*, under date of December 4, 1651, quoted by Bedwell.

[112] Recipe for hipocras: "Take a quart of red wynne, an ounce of cinnamon, and half an ounce of ginger, a quarter of an ounce of greyner and long pepper, and half a pound of sugar, and brose all this (not too small), and then put it into a bage of wollen cloth, made therefore, with the wine, and let it hange over a vessell till the wine be run through." Pitt-Lewis, p. 82, quoting Strutt.

The Temple and Temple Stairs

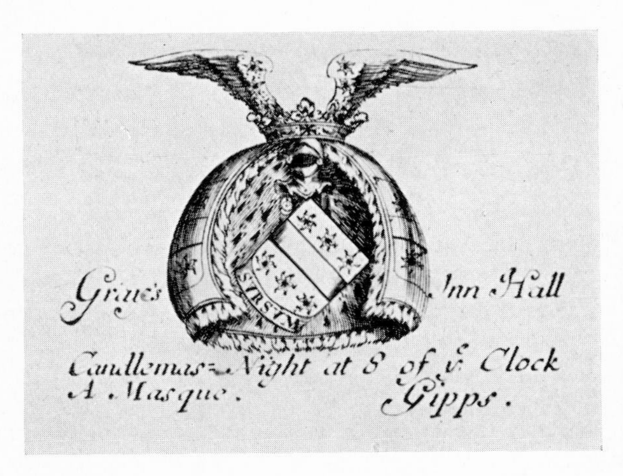

Ticket of Admission to a Masque at Gray's Inn Hall

CHAPTER VII

Miscellaneous Entertainment

A. CREATION OF CHARLES AS PRINCE OF WALES

ON November 4, 1616, when Charles was installed as Prince of Wales, taking the place of Henry,[1] who died shortly before that time, the four Inns of Court were requested to send ten representatives[2] each to contend in the barriers, a mock tournament. Such form of entertainment was considered particularly appropriate for a young prince, especially as Henry had been enthusiastic about military exercise.

At this celebration, which was held in the Banqueting Hall at Whitehall, each of the forty young gentlemen, protected by plate armor, "appoynted in way of honourable combate to breake three staves, three swords, and exchange ten blowes apeece (whose names for their worthinesse I commend to fame)."[3] However, Chamberlain, in writing to Sir Dudley Carleton on November 9, said that the "Ynnes of Court gentlemen carried themselves but indifferently at the barriers," but adds that they recovered their honor at the banquet.[4] William Beecher, in writing to Sir Dudley on the same date, says that the entertainment by the Inns "was much desired and sollicited from the Court and contemptibly censured after the performance."[5]

[1] On Monday, June 4, 1610, the Inns were represented at the investment of Henry as Prince of Wales.

[2] Among those sent by the Inner Temple were Vernon, afterward baron of the exchequer and justice of the King's Bench, and Littleton, later solicitor-general, chief justice of the King's Bench, and lord keeper.

[3] Nichols, *James*, III, 213.

[4] State Papers Dom., Jas. I, Vol. 89, No. 17; quoted in Birch, *James*, I, 436.

[5] State Papers Dom., Jas. I, Vol. 89, No. 15; quoted in Williamson, 270–273.

To defray the expense of this entertainment, an assessment of thirty shillings was made upon every bencher of the Inner Temple, of twenty shillings upon every utter barrister above seven years' standing, of fifteen shillings upon every utter barrister under seven years' standing, and of ten shillings upon all other gentlemen.[6]

B. THE DANCE OF THE NATIONS

ONE of the rather interesting entertainments presented at court soon after the Restoration was a Marathon dance of the nations, if that is not a contradiction of terms, in which gentlemen of Lincoln's Inn, adorned in the costumes of twelve different nations, performed the dances of those nations. The tract describing these dances is entitled, "'Εγκυκλοχρέια or Universal Motion, Being part of that Magnificent Entertainment by the Noble Prince, De la GRANGE, LORD LIEVTENANT OF LINCOLN'S INN, Presented to the high and mighty CHARLES II. Monarck of Great *Brittain*, *France* and *Ireland*. On *Friday* 3 of January 1662. LONDON Printed 1662."[7] The dances follow:

I

A clownish Carrier with a Packet of Books to be distributed by the Master of the Ceremonies, wherein is described the whole designe: he daunceth a Darbishire Round.

II

Gives you a *Bouree*, in the habit of a Thrasonical Gasconian; To let you know, all Frenchmen are not Butterflies.

III

Presents the variety of *Expressions*, made by Motions and Actions of the Body only; For which we are indebted to the Quaker, the last Inventor of Ecclesiastical Postures, who turned Informer, is like to be troublesome to our Assembly.

[6] Inderwick, II, 99.

[7] Reprinted "from a very rare tract in the library" in L. I. Black Book, III, 440.

IV

Shews the truest and most genuine steps of *Ballet.*

V

Two other Clownes with their Lasses, (a double pair of Northern Tikes) who dance a Iigge, the first-born of a Scottish Bagpipe.

VI

Presents you with a *Phantastick Saraband,* manag'd by a Spaniard, To shew a Phantastick Don can be as ridiculous as the most Antick Mounsieur.

VII

Throws you in a Drunkard, with steps proper only to that humor: suitable to the Windmil of his *Pericranium,* which mocions we owe to the lightness of a *Dutchman's* Breeches.

VIII

Gives you a Country Dance, perform'd by *Sheapheards* and *Sheapherdesses,* in the habits of *Arcadian* pastorals; who set forth the Innocency of their minds, by the simplicity of their manners.

IX

Presents a *Corant* single and figured, and a *Saraband serious,* both ascrib'd to the Ingenuity, and *Bon mene* of a well temperd Frenchman.

X

An entry of *Italian Pantaloons;* to shew there are Madmen and Fools in every Countrey, even at *Rome, Paris,* and particularly in *London.*

XI

Presents you (the delight of its age) the *Canaryes,* first invented by the lofty *Italian,* who generally has more wit than honesty.

XII

An entry of *Swises,* who had rather fight than dance, but loves the *Argent* better than both.

A Descant upon the several Movements

Great Sir, y'ave seen Vs, like the active Sun
To please the World, through the whole Zodiac run;
Y'have seen the Noble Spaniard Countermand
All France, with Marches of a Saraband:

And yet with such wise care his Limbs dispose
As if h'ad got the Frenchman in his Hose.

Y'ave seen the Monsieur move, his Arm, Foot, Knee,
And shrugge, as if no Nation danct but he:
His Alamod Corant, his Saraband Pace,
His Bourees; he performd, with the Bon-Grace,

Y'ave seen th'Italian dance the Pantaloon,
No Region wants a Madman or Buffoon!
[The remainder of this stanza has been cut off in binding; it related to the Shepherds.]

The Bonny Scotchman and his merry Lasses,
At Jigge and Bagpipe all the rest surpasses;
What mischief did (that Scotch-witch) Covenant do,
Who charmd the Organs and the bagpipes too?

Most Excellent! active Nations! All put down
The British Bard, sufferd to Act the Clown.
To move the Carriers pace: or Coupee over
With Packets from proud Calais to poor Dover.

And yet nor Seigniour, nor stately Don
Are much above the middle Region:
Tis well in Rome or Spain, if you can see
A handsome Ball once in a Iubilee!

O but the Mounsieur, Englands Dancing Master
Who walks on Parian Marble, Paris-Plaister!
Like th' Element of fire, his spirit soon
Lifts him up to the Concave of the moon.
Dances as soft and nimble as the Aire;
Who vies with him practices to despair!
Dull Englishman is forct to go to France
To change his Cold wear clothes, and learn to dance.

Since t'must be so, weel strike sail and submit,
Wishing the French more Pride, our selves more Wit.
Grand their Minerva, curious, neat, exact,
What ere they can Imagine that dare Act.

Inspir'd with Plumbroth we dance every man,
Save (who eats none) our Presbyterian;
Hee's pardon'd if he move no more, but will
Quietly, with his Good Old Cause, sit still.

Thanks to the Quaker our Last-mover, he
Listed himself into our Company,
Who went good man! to teach the Pope at Rome,
A Babylon slip; the Time yet was not come!

But turn'd our Pursevant, a Lurch, a Pryer;
That wisht the Iesuited knave a Cloyster'd Fryer
Good Saint to shew what weight his Talents beare
Begot a Negro, no Christian you may sweare!
How ere his various postures helpt to prove,
The Brittish Orbe, like other Spheares can move.

England I am sure in former times could dance.
Wittness her many Capers into France.

This entertainment has something in common with the masque; it contains dancing and singing, satire of other countries and of religious denominations within England, as well as of the Puritans, costuming, some setting apparently, and native and Arcadian characters.

CHAPTER VIII

The Drama

A. GORBODUC

ON Twelfth Night, 1561–62, as a part of the Christmas entertainment at the Inner Temple, *Ferrex and Porrex*, the first English tragedy, was presented for the diversion of the lawyers. The unauthorized first edition by William Griffith, dated 1565, says that this tragedy was "shewed before the Queenes most excellent Maiestie in her highness Court of Whitehall the xviii day of January Anno Domini 1561."[1] This statement of the second performance is substantiated by Henry Machyn, whose account,[2] under date of 1561–62, offers an interesting study in both orthography and psychology:

> The xviij day of January was a play[3] in the quen['s] hall at Westmynster by the gentyll-men of the Tempull, and after a grett maske, for ther was a grett skaffold in the hall, with grett tryhumpe as has been sene; and the morow after the skaffold was taken done.

Other unauthorized editions, all of which entitle the play *Gorboduc*, were published in 1565, 1569, 1571, and 1590. The only legitimate edition of the sixteenth century, that of John Daye of 1570, entitled *Ferrex and Porrex*, contains the following address from the printer to the reader:

> Where this Tragedie was for furniture of part of the grand Christmasse in the Inner-Temple, first written about nine yeares agoe by the right honourable Thomas, now Lorde Buckherst, and

[1] January 18, 1561/2 is, of course, January 18, 1562, according to modern computation.

[2] *Diary*, p. 275.

[3] This play is *Ferrex and Porrex*.

by T. Norton, and after shewed before her majestie, and never intended by the Authors thereof to be published: yet one W. G.[4] getting a copie thereof at some yong man's hand that lacked a little money, and much discretion in the last great plage an. 1565, about 5 yeares past, while the said lord was out of England, and T. Norton farre out of London, and neither of them both made privie, put it forth exc*ed*ingly corrupted.

Both Thomas Sackville[5] and Thomas Norton[6] were members of the Inner Temple. The first edition ascribes the first three acts of this play to Norton, and the last two to Sackville. It is interesting that the first English tragedy is one of joint authorship, probably the result of the exigencies of time. Expedition of composition has often demanded collaboration. It is probable, however, that Sackville and Norton were not moved to collaborate by each recognizing a peculiar talent in the other, making assignment of particular portions of the play desirable because of a special ability, as was probably the case in the co-authorship of Beaumont and Fletcher. *Gorboduc*, however, is so thoroughly unified and so unvarying that the transition from one author to the other is scarcely perceptible.

Gorboduc was the first English tragedy to be produced successfully on the stage; it was the response to a demand for dramatic entertainment to form a part of the Christmas celebration. It is possible that, in their desire for variety of entertainment, the gentlemen of the Inner Temple decided to produce a type of drama which had, prior to that time, afforded entertainment only through reading.

Gorboduc is written in blank verse which harmonizes well with the heroic speeches of the characters; it is, however, not especially ductile, and cannot be made to conform to all moods, particularly the lyrical; hence, the uniform cadence

[4] William Griffith.

[5] Sackville was later Lord Buckhurst and eventually the Earl of Dorset.

[6] Norton was a courtier of the queen, and an amateur author.

eventually becomes monotonous. The blank verse used in this play is not an innovation, for Surrey employed it in his translation of the *Aeneid*.

The drama is divided into five acts, a custom which we have almost uniformly observed to the present time. Each of the first four acts closes with a chorus,[7] an importation from the classical drama. Dumb show is used before each act.

Sackville and Norton violate the unity of time, in that the action continues for more than one day, and the unity of place, in that there are frequent changes of scene.

In *Gorboduc* appear numerous stock and straw figures, besides the chorus: the secretaries and counselors and parasites act as does the confidant of classical literature; and Nuntius, or Messenger, of the classics bears the same name in this play.

The source of *Gorboduc*,[8] which has many of the attributes of the Oedipus story, is probably Geoffrey of Monmouth's *History of British Kings*. *Gorboduc*, like *The Misfortunes of Arthur*, is founded on romantic myth surrounding a national hero. Like the Senecans, who went to Greek mythology for dramatic material, Sackville and Norton went to national legend.[9] The similarity of this play to several of those of Shakespeare, and in particular *King Lear*, is too patent to require comment.

The romantic element of *Gorboduc* has, however, been definitely subordinated to political didacticism, which was probably very pleasing to Elizabeth. The play says incontrovertibly that division of rule results in discord; with an appeal for internal placidity, it offers the following picture of national disunion:

[7] Ward, I, 201.

[8] The story of this play is too well known to require recital.

[9] In this respect, *Gorboduc* has had considerable influence on subsequent drama.

One kinsman shall bereave an others life,
The father shall unwitting slay the sonne,
The sonne shall slay the sire and know it not.
Women and maides the cruel souldiers sword
Shall perse to death, and sillie children loe
That playing in the streets and fieldes are found
By violent hand shall close their latter day.

The play closes with the following moral:

For right will alwayes live, and rise at length,
But wrong can never take deepe roote to last.

Sir Philip Sidney says, in his *Defence of Poesie*, that *Gorboduc* is "full of stately speeches and well-sounding phrases . . . and . . . notable morality," and Pope praises the "perspicuity of style" of this play.

Gorboduc must have been rather tenebrous in the midst of the scintillating Christmas entertainment at which the warm heart of Elizabeth dissolved at the very sight of the "tall and proportionable"[10] person of Sir Christopher Hatton, whom she immediately admitted to her group of courtiers. Hatton's grace in dancing acquired for him the sobriquet "the dancing Chancellor." The Poet Gray wrote of him:

Full oft within the spacious walls
When he had fifty summers o'er him,
The grave Lord Keeper led the brawls,
The seal and maces danc'd before him.

His bushy beard and shoe-strings green,
His high-crown'd hat and satin doublet,
Moved the stout heart of England's Queen,
Though Pope and Spaniard could not trouble it.

B. JOCASTA

IN 1566, George Gascoigne, a member of Gray's Inn who devoted the greater part of his time to literature, made, with

[10] Naunton, p. 69; Campbell's *Lives*, II, 140.

the assistance of Francis Kinwelmarsh,[11] an English translation, which they called *Jocasta*, of a play which was thought to be the *Phoenissae* of Euripides. Acts I and IV are usually attributed to Kinwelmarsh and Acts II, III, and V to Gascoigne. Christopher Yelverton, who somewhat later assisted in the composition of the dumb shows for *The Misfortunes of Arthur*, wrote the epilogue for this tragedy, which has the distinction of being the second play written in English in blank verse. Recent scholarship has, however, endeavored to establish that this play was translated directly from the *Giocasta* of M. Lodovico Dolce, and not immediately from the *Phoenissae*.[12] In any event, it was at Gray's Inn that the first known adaptation of a basically Greek play was presented. Here again, even in translation may be found collaboration.

In this play, Gascoigne[13] has retained the Nuntii of the original play. Nuntius became a very important stock character in the early English drama.

Gascoigne, moreover, has employed "dumme shewes and Musickes before every Acte."[14] These dumb shows in the conventional manner forewarn crises to follow. They are of an allegorical nature, like those of *Gorboduc*.

Gascoigne has retained the chorus of "foure Thebane dames."

C. THE SUPPOSES

MORE important in the history of the drama than *Jocasta* is *The Supposes*, a translation in prose by George Gascoigne of *Gli SopposTiti* by Ariosto, said to be, in turn, an adaptation

[11] This name is written "ffrauncis Kynwelmarshe" in the holographic title-page. Kinwelmarsh was also a member of Gray's Inn.

[12] Lawrence, p. 346, and Ward, I, 209; *Modern Philology*, II, 247.

[13] Gascoigne was a descendant of the famous Chief Justice Gascoigne. In 1569 he was commanded to pay his debts to the Inn.

[14] From the quarto.

of the *Captivi* of Plautus and the *Eunuchus* of Terence.[15] *The Supposes* is of great import in that it is the first comedy in prose in the English language. It is, further, the first English comedy presented before an intellectual audience, *Ralph Roister Doister*, by Nicholas Udall, and *Gammer Gurton's Needle*, by William Stevenson, being more elementary productions. *The Supposes*, like *Jocasta*, was presented at the hall at Gray's Inn at some time during 1566. It is the first adaptation in English prose of a play from the Italian, an important source for Shakespeare and other Elizabethans. It, moreover, furnished to Shakespeare inspiration for a secondary plot of *The Taming of the Shrew*.

A prose prologue or argument such as appears in *The Supposes* was an innovation in its day, but prose prologues and epilogues became not uncommon somewhat later.[16] The prologue to *The Supposes* facetiously pretends to explain the title.

D. TANCRED AND GISMUND

THE gentlemen of the Inner Temple, probably in 1568, produced the play *Tancred and Gismund*, another product of collaboration. Act I, which closes, "Finis Actus I. Exegit Rod. Staf.," is still of unknown authorship; Act 2, "Finis Actus 2. Per. Hen: No:" is sometimes ascribed to Henry Noel; Act 3, "Finis Actus 3, G. All.," has not been identified as to authorship; and Act 4, "Finis Actus 4, Composuit Ch: Hat.,"[17] is usually supposed to have been written by Christopher Hatton, who danced his way into Elizabeth's heart. It is believed, however, that Hatton did not act in this play. Act 5, which bears no external mark as to authorship, is usually assigned to Robert Wilmot, who revised and published

[15] Schelling, I, 105.
[16] See the epilogue to *As You Like It*.
[17] Inderwick, I, lxxi, furnishes a lucid account of authorship.

this play in 1592.[18] Manuscripts of the original text of 1568 have been preserved, but there is some divergence between them.[19] For some time after the original production of *Tancred and Gismund*, the manuscript was discarded; even Wilmot spoke of it as "those waste papers." William Webbe, however, considered the play "a most exquisite invention," and prevailed upon Wilmot to publish it. Wilmot thereupon "newly revived and polished" the play "according to the decorum of these daies," by which it has been assumed that he rewrote it in blank verse,[20] and published it with a dedication "To the Worshipful and Learned Society, the GENTLEMEN STUDENTS of the Inner Temple, with the rest of his singular good Friends, the GENTLEMEN of the Middle Temple, and to all other courteous Readers, R. W. wisheth increase of all health, worship, and learning, with the immortal glory of the graces adorning the same." Webbe called the transformation of this play into blank verse "disrobing him of his antique curiosity, and adorning him with the approved guise of our stateliest English terms (not diminishing, but more augmenting his artificial colours of absolute poesy, derived from his first parents)."

Tancred and Gismund is quite as didactic as *Gorboduc*. Robert Wilmot, in his dedication to "the Right Worshipful Ladies, the Lady MARY PETER and the Lady ANNE GRAY," says: "I devised this way with myself to procure the same, persuading myself, there is nothing more welcome to your wisdoms than the knowledge of wise, grave, and worthy matters, tending to the good instructions of youths, of whom

[18] This date is sometimes given as 1591. It was probably printed between January and March 15, 1591/2, which would be 1592 according to modern computation.

[19] MS, Lansdowne 786, probably written from 1568 to 1570, and Hargrave MS 205, which is much more modern. (See Hazlitt, *Old English Plays*.) Part of the original was found in a chest of Mr. Powell, Milton's father-in-law.

[20] Thus the standard established by *Gorboduc* was followed.

Sir Christopher Hatton

you are mothers," and, in another place,[21] he says that his purpose, "tendeth only to the exaltation of virtue and suppression of vice, with pleasure to profit and help all men, but to offend or hurt no man."

Tancred and Gismund, which in tone resembles Gascoigne's *Jocasta* and in being inspired by Italian literature resembles Gascoigne's *Supposes*, is said to have been taken from Boccaccio's *Decameron* (day fourth, novel first).[22] It will be recalled that, about a hundred years later, Dryden published his version of the same story.[23] *Tancred and Gismund*[24] is said to be the oldest extant tragedy the source of which is an Italian *novella*.[25]

This play, which is divided into acts like the first English tragedy, is more melodramatic than *Gorboduc*; it is, nevertheless, of greater literary value. Like *Gorboduc*, each act opens with a premonitory dumb show, but in *Tancred and Gismund* this pantomime is more an integral part of the play. The chorus is similar to that of *Gorboduc*.

A considerable amount of Italian machinery seems to have been used in the production of this play. The conclusion indicates that a curtain concealed the stage from the audience.[26] Moreover, the Furies rise from hell, just as in *Gorboduc*, apparently with the aid of a machine. At the opening of the play, Cupid, a "naked boy, not cloth'd but with . . . wings," is precipitated from heaven in a similar manner.

It is with the entrance of Cupid that the semblance of the stage direction is found, as well as close similarity to the

[21] As a continuation of the dedication to the Inner Temple.

[22] See Hazlitt, *Old English Plays*.

[23] *Fables*, "Segismonda and Guiscardo." Note similarity to the works of Lope de Vega and Calderón, of Spanish literature.

[24] This play was called *Gismonde of Salerne* when presented at the Temple. Chambers (*Eliz. Stage*, iii, 514) thinks that this play may have been produced at Greenwich in 1567.

[25] A source employed considerably by Shakespeare.

[26] Creizenach, p. 362. The curtain was not used in Greek productions.

masque: "CUPID cometh out of the heavens in a cradle of flowers, drawing forth upon the stage, in a blue twist of silk, from his left hand, Vain Hope, Brittle Joy: and with a carnation twist of silk from his right hand, Fair Resemblance, Late Repentance."

Tancred and Gismund will be recalled with a quotation of the argument:

> TANCRED, the Prince of Salerne, overloves
> His only daughter (wonder of that age)
> Gismund, who loves the County[27] Palurin
> Guiscard, who quites her likings with his love:
> A letter in a cane describes the means
> Of their two meetings in a secret cave.
> Unconstant fortune leadeth forth the king
> To this unhappy sight, wherewith in rage
> The gentle earl he doometh to his death,
> And greets his daughter with her lover's heart.
> Gismunda fills the goblet with her tears,
> And drinks a poison which she had distill'd,
> Whereof she dies, whose deadly countenance
> So grieves her father, that he slew himself.

Tancred and Gismund, although well written, offers little innovation. It rather closely follows the fashion set by *Gorboduc*. Its chief individuality probably lies in the fact that it is a blending of elements from the Greek, the Roman, and the Italian drama.

E. THE MISFORTUNES OF ARTHUR

The Misfortunes of Arthur, produced at Greenwich by the gentlemen of Gray's Inn during the "thirtieth yeare of her Majesties most happie Raigne,"[28] is also the product of collaboration. However, the incoherence which was likely to

[27] A nobleman.

[28] February 28, 1588. See title-page of 1587 edition by Robert Robinson. (Probably printed in early March, 1587/8.)

result from joint authorship was beginning to be recognized in 1588. In the composition of *The Misfortunes of Arthur*, therefore, Thomas Hughes was assigned the duty of writing the tragedy proper; thus a unity difficult to obtain in a play divided among several persons was procured. However, to seven assistants was committed the composition of various dramatic ornamentations: Nicholas Trotte[29] wrote the introduction, marked by legal *jeu d'esprit;* William Fulbeck wrote two substitutional speeches; Francis Flower wrote the rhymed choruses for the first and second acts; Christopher Yelverton, John Lancaster, and Francis Bacon, then twenty-six and recently admitted to the bench, composed the dumb shows; and Penruddock, aided by Flower and Lancaster, "directed the proceedings at court."[30]

Like *Gorboduc*, *The Misfortunes of Arthur* is the result of the blending of material from the Senecan drama and domestic legend. The source of *The Misfortunes of Arthur* is probably not, as has often been said,[31] the *Morte d'Arthur*, but the *History* of Geoffrey of Monmouth,[32] which is also the source of *Gorboduc*. Hughes, then, turned to native legendary material much as the Senecans turned to Greek mythological sources. He was continuing a practice begun by Sackville and Norton, a practice well known to Shakespeare, who constantly resorted to Holinshed. Hughes was, however, the first of the dramatists to make use of the Arthurian romance, which was employed by several Elizabethans.[33] *The Misfortunes of Arthur* is more directly the precursor of the Elizabethan historical play than is *Gorboduc*.

The Misfortunes of Arthur follows the tradition of

[29] Sometimes Trotter.

[30] Preface to nineteenth century edition by J. P. Collier.

[31] Ward, I, 218.

[32] Grumbine, p. 32.

[33] For example, *The Birth of Merlin*, attributed to Shakespeare and Rowley.

tragedy in that it is written in blank verse,[34] which seems, in nearly thirty years, to have become more mobile. Even in 1588, however, it is somewhat monotonous, especially in the wordplays and quibbles, which are numerous. Moreover, alliteration in *The Misfortunes of Arthur* makes the blank verse somewhat unpleasant.

The chorus and the dumb shows, especially the rise of the Furies, as in *Gorboduc* and *Tancred and Gismund*, are entirely conventional, as are the nymphs (a link between the masque and the tragedy), and Nuntius. The arguments of the dumb shows foreshadow the modern stage direction. *The Misfortunes of Arthur* is divided into five acts, in accordance with custom. The unities are violated, as they are in earlier English tragedies. One of the innovations of *The Misfortunes of Arthur* is the introduction of the ghost, much like Tantalus of Seneca's *Thyestes* and Polydorus of Euripides' *Hecuba*.[35] In a sense, Hughes's ghost is an ancestor of the creations of Kyd and Shakespeare.

Like the earlier English tragedies, *The Misfortunes of Arthur* is tinged with moralizing. The introduction says that the play will recount "In tragic notes the plagues of vice." Among the better specimens of this intention are the following:

> Tongues are untam'd and fame is envy'd dog,
> That absent barks, and present fawns as fast.

> . . . though death redeem us all from foes
> . . . yet death redeems us not from tongues.

> Besides, fame's but a blast that sounds awhile,
> And quickly stints, and then is quite forgot.

[34] There are two exceptions to this statement; in one case, a rhyme closes a speech, perhaps to give heroic finality. Shakespeare sometimes uses a heroic couplet in terminating a speech.

[35] Grumbine, pp. 10–22, offers a good account of the ghost.

Such epigrammatic style is probably derived from the classics, in which Hughes, and probably all his assistants, was a scholar. The moral of *Gorboduc* is, however, more potent because it more directly concerns the mode of living and the system of government. Hughes seems to have difficulty in warming the somewhat frigid Arthurian legend in a Senecan alembic.

The Misfortunes of Arthur is, then, like *Gorboduc* and *Tancred and Gismund,* one of the important English tragedies of the Senecan type. In fact, a great part of this play seems to be a blending of material from the classical drama. *The Misfortunes of Arthur* probably is suffused with more Greek tincture, as adopted by Seneca, than is any other tragedy of the sixteenth century, for Hughes probably knew more about Greek literature in the original than did his colleagues. This play, unlike its predecessors, introduces, in a sort of preliminary masque, much of the atmosphere of the law court. Its principal importance, however, probably lies in the fact that it presented to the theater for the first time the Arthurian legend.

F. MISCELLANEOUS PLAYS

FROM 1650 to the end of the century, numerous plays were presented by professional actors at the Inns of Court. The records of the Inner Temple,[36] though frequently noting the amount paid "for a play," sometimes give the name of the play, and, less often, the name of the author. The following list, which is not intended to be complete for even the Inner Temple, may indicate that the play presented at any of the Inns was usually of a popular nature:

1582, *Damon and Pithias,* by Richard Edwards, of Lincoln's Inn. This play, printed in 1582, was presented by the children of

[36] F. A. Inderwick's *Calendar of Inner Temple Records* has been indispensable in the compilation of this list.

the chapel before Elizabeth in 1571. In accordance with custom, this play was probably originally produced at Lincoln's Inn.

1594, December 28: *The Comedy of Errors*, probably Shakespeare's play. Gray's Inn hall.

1601, February: *Twelfth Night*, by Shakespeare. Middle Temple hall.

1608, February 2: *The Oxford Tragedy;* thought by Inderwick to be *The Yorkshire Tragedy*, sometimes incorrectly attributed to Shakespeare. Inner Temple hall.

1610, *The Fleire*, by Edward Sharpham of the Middle Temple; probably presented in the Middle Temple hall. 1610 is the date of publication.

1657, November 5: *The Countryman*, by William Davenant. Inner Temple hall. About December 4, 1657, the same play was acted in the Middle Temple hall.

1659, November 23, or thereabout: *The Clown.* Middle Temple hall. The same record includes payment for *Wit without Money*, acted November 2.

1663, November 2: *The Brothers*, by James Shirley. Inner Temple hall. Typical Spanish plot, including references to the defeat of the armada.

1664, February 2: *Epicene, or The Silent Woman*, by Ben Jonson, presented in the Inner Temple hall by His Majesty's Players. For the Restoration revival, Dryden wrote a prologue and an epilogue.

1664, November 1: *The Night Walker, or The Little Thief*, by Beaumont and Fletcher. Presented by His Majesty's Players in the Inner Temple hall.

1665, February 2: *The Changes, or Love in a Maze*, by James Shirley. This play, acted by the King's Players in the Inner Temple hall, has a countryman as one of its chief characters. Plays in which the city gentleman is contrasted to the bumpkin seem to have been as popular at the Inns as elsewhere. This play, which Pepys thought dull and silly, should not be confused with Boucicault's more successful play of this name.

1669, February 2: *The Comical Revenge, or Love in a Tub*, by George Etherege. Acted by "the players of the Duke's house" at the Inner Temple hall. This sentimental play, largely in verse, includes low comedy, in which a French valet, in Diogenes fashion, walks about the stage with a tub encircling his body. Betterton and his wife played the principal rôles.

1669, *Secret Love or the Maiden Queen*, by John Dryden. Acted by "the King's players" in the Inner Temple hall. This play, in blank verse and rhyme, was very popular. The plot is said to have been suggested to Dryden by the king, who called it his play. Pepys highly commended the acting of Nell Gwyn in the part of Florimel.

1669, *The Little French Lawyer*, by Beaumont and Fletcher. Presented in the Inner Temple hall by the King's Players. The students probably found pleasing the chief characters, who are lawyers fighting a duel.

1670, November 1: *Sir Martin Mar-all*, by John Dryden. This play, acted by the Duke's Players in the Inner Temple hall, is an adaptation of Molière's *L'Étourdi*. Pepys considered "mighty witty" the rather low comedy of this play.

1671, February 2: *The Committee*, by Robert Howard, brother-in-law of John Dryden. Presented by the King's Players at the Inner Temple hall, at which time the king was the guest of the treasurer. This play, dealing with the sequestration of estates during the Commonwealth, was produced again in February, 1685/6, and on February 2, 1670/1, at the Inner Temple.

1671, November 1: *Philaster, or Love Lyes a Bleeding*, by Beaumont and Fletcher. Acted by the King's Players at the Inner Temple hall. Nell Gwyn was one of the actors.

1675, November 1: *The Scornful Lady*, by Beaumont and Fletcher. Acted by the King's Players in the Inner Temple hall.

1676, February 2: *The Spanish Curate*, by Beaumont and Fletcher. This play, probably with a Spanish source, was acted by the King's Players at the Inner Temple hall. On November 1, 1686, it was reproduced at the Inner Temple.

1682, February 2: *London Cuckolds*, by Edward Ravenscroft, a member of the Middle Temple. This play, one of the many which figured in the city-country controversy of the time, depreciates the city. It was very inappropriately acted before the lord Chancellor and the judges in the Inner Temple hall by the Duke's Players. Because of its licentious nature, the actresses later refused to act in it; Garrick declined to present it in his theater.

1682, November 1: *Rule a Wife and Have a Wife*, by Beaumont and Fletcher. Presented by the Duke's Players in the Inner Temple hall. The source of this play is said to be that of Shakespeare's *The Taming of the Shrew*.

1683, November 1: *The Plain Dealer*, by William Wycherley. Presented by the Duke's Players in the Inner Temple hall. The sources of this play are probably Molière's *Le Misanthrope* and Shakespeare's *Twelfth Night*. The dedication to a "procuress and plain-dealer" is very amusing. Wycherley was a member of the Inner Temple.

1684, November 1: *The Fond Husband, or The Plotting Sisters*, by Tom Durfey. Presented by the Duke's Players at the Inner Temple hall. This play was very popular; Charles II was among the audience on three of the first five nights of its presentation.

1685, November 4: *The Soldier's Fortune*, by Thomas Otway. Performed by "Mr. Davenant's players" (the Duke's Players) at the Inner Temple hall. This somewhat vulgar play was naturally very popular.

1687, February 2: *The Spanish Friar*, by John Dryden. This play, often called *The Spanish Priest*, was performed by the Duke's Players at the Inner Temple. It will be recalled that, by order of James II, it was not permitted on the stage because of its reflections upon Roman Catholicism, and that it was the first one called for by Queen Mary.

1687, November 1: *The Cheats of Scapin*, by Thomas Otway. This play, presented in the Inner Temple hall, by the Duke's Players, is an adaptation of *Les Fourberies de Scapin*, by Molière.

This list is sufficient to show the nature of the play which was popular at the Inns of Court. The works of Beaumont and Fletcher seem to have been especially favored. It will be noted that the sources of several of these plays are in French and Spanish literature.

With the rapid development of the professional drama in the seventeenth century, the amateur productions of the Inns of Court began to fall into desuetude. During the second half of the century the iridescent masque began to vanish, and the play composed by young lawyers was discarded. The apparent lack of interest of the legal profession in dramatic production at this time may be accounted for not only by the fact that professional dramatists and producers could create superior plays, but that the age was becoming one of specialization: the parliaments, the council, and the pension at the Inns were beginning to circumscribe Christmas festivities, for which numerous masques and plays were composed. In accordance with the spirit of the age, the law student began to confine himself to the law, the dramatist to the drama.

Appendices

APPENDIX A[1]

(Public Record Office, State Papers Domestic, Elizabeth, Vol. XCV, No. 91)

"A survey of the chambers and societies of all the Innes of Courte together with certain devyses for the government of the worthie and necessarie sorte and for the exclusion of the unworthie and unnecessarie number and sorte thereof. Maie, 1574.

THE SURVEY TOWCHINGE THE PREMISES

LINCOLN'S INNE.

The number of chambers there:—iiij^{xx}xij.

The number of fellowes there of all these sortes following, viz:—

Benchers	xiij	clx whereof	having chambers, cxxx
Utter barristers	xxxij		having no chambers, xxx.
Other gentlemen	cxvij		

GRAIES INNE.

The number of chambers there:—cxxiiij.

The number of fellowes there of all these sortes following, viz:—

Benchers	xij	ccxx whereof	havinge chambers, cciiij
Utter barristers	xxx		havinge no chambers, xvj$^{en.}$
Other gentlemen	clxxviij		

THE INNER TEMPLE.

The number of chambers there:—c.

The number of fellowes there of all these sortes followinge, viz:—

Benchers	xv	ciiij^{xx}ix whereof	havinge chambers, clxiij.
Utter barristers	xxiij		havinge no chambers, xxvj.
Other gentlemen	clj		

[1] Reproduced in Inderwick, I, Appendix No. III, 468.

THE MIDDLE TEMPLE.

The number of chambers there, lxxxxij.

The number of fellowes there of all these sortes followinge, viz:—

Benchers	xj	ciiij^{xx}x whereof	havinge chambers, cxxx.
Utter barristers	xl		havinge no chambers, lx.
Other gentlemen	cxxxix^{en}		

51 (benchers)	759	627 [having chambers].
125 (utter barristers)		132 [having no chambers]."
593 (other gentlemen)		

APPENDIX B

Typical List of Gifts of Newly Created Sergeants[1]

"First to the Quenes heighnes a Ringe of vi l. xiii s. iiii d. for them all in Common. *Lex Regis praefidium*, were the words in the Ring.

Item the Lorde Keeper of the greate Seale, a Ringe of xviii s. of everie new Serjaunt.

Item the Lorde Treafurer a like Ringe of every new Serjaunt.

Item the Lorde Steward a like Ringe of everye of them.

Item the Lorde Privye Seale the like.

Item the Lorde great Chamberlayne a like Ringe of everye of them.

Item the Lorde greate Mafter likewife.

Item the Lorde Chamberlayne of the Quenes Houfeholde a like Ringe of everie of them.

Item the two cheefe Juftices like Rings of everye of them.

Item the Cheeffe Steward of that feafte, a Ringe of xx s. of them all in Common.

Item the Comptrowler, one like Ringe of them all in Common.

Item the Marfhall, one Ringe of xii s. of them all in Common.

Item to the Warden of the Fleete, one like Ringe of them all in Common.

Item the Maifter of Rolls, a Ringe of xvi s. of everye of them.

Item to everye other Juftice of both Benches a Like Ringe of everye of them.

Item to the two Cheeffe Secretaries, like Rings of everye of them.

Item to everye of the olde three Serjaunts, of every of thofe newe Serjaunts, a Ringe of xii s.

Item to the Quenes Attorney a Ringe of xii s. of everye of them.

Item to the Quenes Solycyter one Ringe of like valewe of everye of them.

Item to two Clarkes of the Crowne, everye of them one Ringe of v s. of everye of them.

[1] From Dugdale, pp. 124–127.

Item to the three Barons of Th'exchequer, everye of them one Ringe of everye Serjaunt of x s. a piece.

Item to the three Prothonotaries of the Common place of everye of them one Ringe, price v s. a peece.

Item to the Clarke of the Warrants, one like Ringe of everye of them.

Item to the Cirographer one like Ringe of everye of them.

Item to the Prothonotarye of the Kings Benche, of everye of them one Ringe, price v s.

Item to the xv. Filacers and Exegenters to everye of them a Ringe of ll s. vi d. the peece of everye of them.

Item to the Clarke of the Councell, of everye of them a Ringe of the like valewe.

Item to the *Custos Brevium* of everye of them one Ringe of the like valewe.

Item to as manie Attorneys as they will, Rings.

Item, manie Rings to other ſeveral friends.

The Common liveryes geven by thoſe newe Serjaunts.

Firſte to ther heighe Steward fowre xls. yeards of x s. the yearde	xls.
Item to his fowre ſervants, vi. yeards, at vi s. the yearde	xxxvi s.
Item to the Comptrowler iiii yeards, at x s. the yearde	xls.
Item to fowre of his ſervants, vi. yeards, at vi s. the yearde	xxxvi s.
Item to the Cheeffe Marſhall iiii yeards, at xs. the yearde	xls.
Item to the Warden of the Fleete, iiii. yeardes at x s. the yearde	xls.
Item to his viii. ſervants, xii yeards at vi s. the yearde	iii l. xii s.
Item to the Marſhall of the Exchequer, iii. yeardes, at viii s. the yearde	xxiiii s.
Item to the Marſhall of the Common place iii. yeards at vi s the yearde	xviii s.
Item to the Lorde Cheeffe Juſtice of the Kings	

Benche iiii. ſervants, vi. yeards, at vi s. the yearde . . xxxvi s.

Item to the Lorde Cheeffe Juſtice of the Common place, fowre ſervants, vi. yeards, at vi s. the yearde . . xxxvi s.

Item to the Lorde Cheeffe Baron of the Exchequer iiii ſervants . . . . xxxvi s.

Item to everye Juſtice of everye Benche thre ſervants, iiii yeards and a half, at vi s. the yearde . . . . xxvii s.

Item to everye olde Serjaunts two ſervants, iii. yeards, at vi ſhillings the yearde . . . . xviii s.

Item to iiii. Uſhers of Th'exchequer, xii. yeards at vi. s. the yearde . . . . iii l. xii s.

Item to one of the Tenn Porters, one yearde & dim. the yearde . . . . ix s.

Item to the Keeper of Serjaunts Inne in Chancery Lane, two yeards, at vi s. the yearde . . . . . xii s.

Item to the Bokebearer of the Common place, one yearde & dim. at vi s. the yearde . . . . . . ix s.

Item to the ſix Butlers, xviii yeards, at vi s. the yearde v l. viii s.

Item to the fower Cryers of the Common place, ix. yeards, at vi s. the yearde . . . . Liiii s.

Item to the Marſhall of the Kings Benche, iii. yeards, at vi s. the yearde . . . . xviii s.

Item to the Cryer of the Chancery, iii yeards at vi s. the yearde . . . . xviii s.

Item to the Porter of the Chancery, one yearde & dimidum, at vi s. the yearde . . . . ix s.

Item to the Cryer of the Kings Benche, iii. yeards at vi s. the yearde . . . . xviii s.

Item to the Porter of the Kings Benche, one yearde and a halfe, at vi s. the yearde . . . . ix s.

Item to the Dreſſer of the Common place, one yearde and an halfe . . . . ix s.

Item to the Porter of the Common place, 3. yeards, vi s. the yearde . . . . xviii s.

Item to the Steward and Buttlers of the Myddle Temple, xii. yeards, vi s. the yearde . . . . . . iii l. xii s.

Item to the Steward and Butlers of the Inner Temple, xii. yeards, at vi s. the yearde . . . . . . iii l. xii s.

Item to the Steward and Butlers of Lincoln's Inne, xii. yeards, at vi s. the yearde . . . . iii l. xii s.

Item to the Steward and Butlers of Grayes Inne, xii yeards at vi s. the yearde . . . . iii l. xii s.

Item to the Clarke of the Kitchen, and his two men, vi. yeards at vi s. the yearde . . . . xxxvi s.

Item to three Porters, iii yeards & dim. at vi s. the yearde . . . . xxvii s.

Item to the Cheeffe Porter, iii. yeards at vi. s. the yearde . . . . xviii s."

APPENDIX C

Officers at Celebration of Grand Christmas, 1561-2, at Inner Temple

(From *The Progresses and Public Processions of Queen Elizabeth &c.*, by John Nichols, I, 131)

"Mr. Onslow, Lord Chancellour.
Anthony Stapleton, Lord Treasurer.
Robert Kelway, Lord Privy Seal.
John Fuller, Chief Justice of the King's Bench.
William Pole, Chief Justice of the Common Pleas.
Roger Manwood, Chief Baron of the Exchequer.
Mr. Bashe, Steward of the Household.
Mr. Copley, Marshall of the Household.
Mr. Paten, Chief Butler.
Christopher Hatton, Master of the Game. [He was afterward Lord Chancellour of England.]

Mr. Blaston,
Mr. Yorke,
Mr. Penston,
Mr. Jervise, } Masters of the Revells.

Mr. Parker, Lieutenant of the Tower.
Mr. Kendall, Carver.
Mr. Martyn, Ranger of the Forests.
Mr. Stradling, Sewer.
And there were fourscore of the Guard; besides divers others not here named."

APPENDIX D

Officers at Celebration of Grand Christmas, 1594-5, at Gray's Inn

(From *The Progresses and Public Processions of Queen Elizabeth, &c.*, by John Nichols, III, 265)

"A Marshal. A Marshal.

Trumpets. Trumpets.

Pursuevant at Arms, *Layne*.

Townsmen in the Prince's Livery, with halberts.

Yeomen of the Guard, three couples.

Captain of the Guard, *Grimes*.

Baron of the Grand Port, *Dudley*.

Baron of the Petty Port, *Williams*.

Baron of the Base Port, *Grante*.

Baron of the New Port, *Lovel*.

Gentlemen for Entertainment, three couples, *Binge*, &c.

Gentlemen for Entertainment, three couples, *Wentworth*, *Zukendeu*, *Forrest*.

Lieutenant of the Pensioners, *Tonstal*.

Gentlemen Pensioners, twelve couples, *viz.*

Lawson. *Rotts.* *Davison.*

Devereux. *Anderson.*

Stapleton. *Glascott.* *cum reliquis.*

Daniel. *Elken.*

Chief Ranger, and Master of the Game, *Forrest*.

Master of the Revels, *Lambert*.

Master of the Revellers, *Tevery*.

Captain of the Pensioners, *Cooke*.

Sewer, *Archer*.

Carver, *Moseley*.

Another Sewer, *Drewry*.

Lord Chief Justice of the Prince's Bench, *Crew*.

Master of the Ordnance, *Fitz-Williams*.

Lieutenant of the Tower, *Lloyd*.

Master of the Jewel-house, *Darlen*.

Treasurer of the Household, *Smith*.

Knight Marshal, *Bell*.

Sheriff, *Leach*.

Clerk of the Council, *Jones*.
Clerk of the Parliament.
Clerk of the Crown, *Downes*.
Orator, *Heke*.
Recorder, *Starkey*.
Solicitor, *Dunne*.
Serjeant, *Goldsmith*.
Speaker of the Parliament, *Bellen*.
Commissary, *Greenwood*.
Attorney, *Holt*.
Serjeant, *Hitchcombe*.
Master of the Requests, *Faldo*.
Chancellor of the Exchequer, *Kitts*
Master of the Wards and Idiots, *Ellis*.
Reader, *Cobb*.
Lord Chief Baron of the Exchequer, *Briggs*.
Master of the Rolls, *Hetlen*.
Lord Chief Baron of the Common Pleas, *Damporte*.
The Shield of Pegasus,[1] for the Inner Temple, *Scevington*.
Serjeant at Arms with the Sword, *Glascott*
Gentleman Usher, *Paylor*.
The Shield of the Griffin,[1] for Gray's-Inn, *Wickliffe*.
The King at Arms, *Perkinson*.
The Great Shield of the Prince's Arms, *Cobley*.
Master of the Wardrobe, *Conney*.
Comptroller of the Household, *Bouthe*.
Bishop of St. Giles in the Fields, *Dandye*.
Steward of the Household, *Smith*.
Lord Warden of the Four Ports, *Damporte*.
Secretary of State, *Jones*.
Lord Admiral, *Cecill* (*Richard*).
Lord Treasurer, *Morrey*.
Lord Great Chamberlain, *Southworth*.
Lord High Constable.
Lord Marshal, *Knaplock*.
Lord Privy Seal, *Lamphew*.
Lord Chamberlain of the Household, *Markham*.
Lord High Steward, *Kempe*.
Lord Chancellor, *Johnson*.
Archbishop of St. Andew's in Holborn, *Bush*.
Serjeant at Arms with the Mace, *Flemming*.
Gentleman Usher, *Chevett*.
The Prince of Purpoole, *Helmes*
A Page of Honour, *Wannforde*.
Gentlemen of the Privy Chamber, six couples.
A Page of Honour, *Butler* (*Roger*).

[1] These shields, like the dedication to the *Gesta Grayorum* and the invitation of the gentlemen of Gray's to the gentlemen of the Inner Temple to attend the Christmas celebration of 1594–95, testify to the ancient friendship of these two houses.

Vice-Chamberlain, *Butler* (*Thomas*).

Master of the Horse, *Fitz-Hugh.*

Yeomen of the Guards, three couples.

Townsmen in Liveries.

The Family and Followers."

APPENDIX E

Address of the Prince of Purpoole and Replies of his Six Councillors at Christmas Celebration at Gray's Inn, 1594-5, Supposedly Written by Francis Bacon

(From *The Progresses and Public Processions of Queen Elizabeth, &c.*, by John Nichols, III, 287, *et seq.*)

"My Lords,

"We have made choice of you, as our most faithful and favoured Counsellors, to advise with you, not any particular action of our State, but in general, of the scope and end whereunto you think it most for our honour, and the happiness of our State, that our government be rightly bent and directed; for we mean not to do as many Princes use; which conclude of their ends out of their own honours, and take counsel only of the means (abusing, for the most part, the wisdom of their Counsellors) set them the right way to the wrong place. But we, desirous to leave as little to chance or humour as may be, do now give you liberty and warrant to set before us, to what port, as it were, the ship of our government should be bounden. And this we require you to do, without either respect to our affections, or your own; neither guessing what is most agreeable with our disposition, wherein we may easily deceive you; for Princes' hearts are inscrutable: nor, on the other side, putting the case by yourselves, as if you would present us with a robe, whereof measure were taken by yourselves. Thus you perceive our mind, and we expect your answer."

The First Counsellor advising the Exercise of War.

"Most Excellent Prince,

"Except there be such amongst us, as I am fully persuaded there is none, that regardeth more his own greatness under you, than your great (*sic*) over others, I think there will be little difference in the chusing for you a goal worthy your vertue and power. For he that shall set before him your magnanimity and valour, supported by the youth and disposition of your body; your flourishing Court, like the horse of *Troy*, full of brave commanders and leaders; your populous and man-rife provinces, overflowing with warlike people; your coffers, like the Indian mines when that they are first opened; your store-houses are as sea-walls, like the Vulcan's cave; your navy like to an huge floating city; the devotion of your subjects to your crown and person, their good agreement amongst themselves, their wealth and provision: and then your strength and unrevocable confederation with the noble and honourable personages, and the fame and reputation without of so rare a concurrence, whereof all the former regards do grow: how can he think any exercise worthy of your means, but that of conquest? for, in few words, what is your strength, if you find it not? Your fortune, if you try it not? Your vertue, if you show it not? Think, excellent Prince, what sense of content you found in yourself when you were first invested in our state: for though I know your Excellency is far from vanity and lightness, yet it is the nature of all things to find rest when they come to due and proper places. But be assured of this, that this delight will languish and vanish; for power will quench appetite, and satiety will endure tediousness. But if you embrace the wars, your trophies and triumphs will be as continual coronations that will not suffer your glory and contentment to fade and wither. Then, when you have enlarged your territories, ennobled your country, distributed fortunes, good or bad, at your pleasure, not only to particulars, but to cities and nations; marked the computations of time with your expeditions and voyages, and the memory of places by your exploits and victories, in your later years you shall find a sweet respect into the adventures of your youth, you shall enjoy your reputation, you shall record your travels, and after your own time you shall eternize your name, and leave deep footsteps of your power in the world. To conclude, excellent Prince, and most worthy to have the titles of victories added to your high and deserved titles: remember, the Divines find nothing more glorious to resemble our state unto than warfare. All things in earnest and jest do affect a kind of victory, and all other victories are but shadows to the victories of the wars. Therefore embrace the wars, for they disparage you not; and believe, that if any Prince do otherwise, it is either in the weakness of his mind or means."

The Second Counsellor, advising the Study of Philosophy.

"It may seem, Most Excellent Prince, that my Lord, which now hath spoken, did never read the just censures of the wisest men, who compared great conquerors to great rovers and witches, whose power is in destruction, and not in preservation; else would he never have advised your Excellency to become as some comet, or blazing-star, which would threaten and portend nothing but death and dearth, combustions and troubles of the world. And whereas the governing faculties of men are two, force and reason; whereof the one is brute, and the other divine, he wisheth you for your principal ornament and regality, the talons of the eagle to catch the prey, and not the piercing sight which seeth into the bottom of the sea: but I, contrarywise, will wish unto your Highness the exercise of the best and purest part of the mind, and the most innocent and meriting request, being the conquest of the works of nature; making his proportion, that you bend the excellency of your spirits to the searching out, inventing, and discovering of all whatsoever is hid in secret in the world, that your Excellency be not as a lamp that shineth to others, and yet seeth not itself; but as the eye of the world, that both carrieth and useth light. Antiquity, that presenteth unto us in dark visions the wisdom of former times, informeth us, that the kingdoms have always had an affinity with the secrets and mysteries of learning. Amongst the Persians, the Kings were attended on by the Magi; the Gymnosophists had all the government under the Princes of Asia; and generally those kingdoms were accounted most happy, that had rulers most addicted to philosophy: the Ptolemies of Egypt may be for instance; and Solyman was a man so seen in the universality of nature, that he wrote an herbal of all that was green upon the earth. No conquest of Julius Caesar made him so remembered as the Calendar. Alexander the Great wrote to Aristotle upon the publishing of the Physicks, that he esteemed more of excellent men in knowledge, than in empire. And to this purpose I will commend to your Highness four principal works and monuments of yourself: First, the collecting of a most perfect and general library, wherein whatsoever the wit of man hath heretofore committed to books of worth, be they ancient or modern, printed or manuscript, European or of the other parts, of one or other language, may be made contributary to your wisdom. Next, a spacious, wonderful garden, wherein whatsoever plant, the sun of divers climates, out of the earth of divers moulds, either wild, or by the culture of man, brought forth, may be, with that care that appertaineth to the good prospering thereof, set and cherished. This garden to be built about with rooms, to stable in all rare beasts, and to cage in all rare birds; with two lakes adjoining, the one of fresh water, and the other of salt, for like variety of fishes: and so you may have, in a small compass, a model of universal nature made private. The third a goodly huge cabinet, wherein whatsoever the hand of man, by exquisite art or engine, hath made rare in stuff, form, or motion, whatsoever singularity, chance, and the shuffle of things hath produced, whatsoever nature hath wrought in things that want life, and may be kept, shall be sorted and included. The fourth, such a Still-house so furnished with mills, instruments, furnaces, and vessels, as may be a Palace fit for a philosopher's stone. Thus when your Excellency shall have added depth of knowledge to the fineness of spirits, and greatness of your power, then indeed shall you lay a Trismegistus; and then, when all other miracles and wonders shall cease, by reason that you shall have discovered their natural causes, yourself shall be left the only miracle and wonder of the world."

The Third Counsellor, advising Eternizement and Fame, by Buildings and Foundations.

"My Lords that have already spoken, most excellent Prince, have both used one fallacy, in taking that for certain and granted, which was most uncertain and doubtful: for the one hath neither drawn in question the success and fortune of the wars; nor the other, the difficulties and errors in the conclusions of nature: but these immoderate hopes and promises do many times issue from those of the wars, into tragedies of calamities and distresses; and those of mystical philosophy, into comedies of ridiculous frustrations and disappointments of such conceipts and curiosities: but, on the other side, in one point my Lords have well agreed, that they both, according to their several intentions, counselled your Excellency to win fame, and to eternize your name; though the one adviseth it in a course of great peril, and the other, of little dignity and magnificence. But the plain and approved way that is safe, and yet proportionable to the greatness of a Monarch, to present himself to posterity, is not rumour and hear-say; but the usual memory of himself, is the magnificence of goodly and Royal buildings and foundations, and the new institutions of orders, ordinances, and societies: that is, that your coin be stamped with your own image; so in every part of your State there may be somewhat new; which by continuance may make the founder and author remembered. It was perceived at the first, when men sought to cure mortality by fame, that buildings was the only way; and thereof proceeded the known holy antiquity of building the Tower of Babel; which, as it was a sin in the immoderate appetite of fame, so was it punished in the kind; for the diversities of languages have imprisoned fame ever since. As for the pyramids, the colosses, the number of temples, colleges, bridges, aqueducts, castles, theatres, palaces, and the like, they may shew us, that men ever mistrusted any other way to fame than this only, of works and monuments. Yea, even they which had the best choice of other means. Alexander did not think his fame so engraven in his conquests, but that he thought it further shined in the buildings of Alexandria. Augustus Caesar thought no man had done greater things in military actions than himself; yet that which, at his death, ran most in his mind, was his buildings; when he said, not as some mistake it, metaphorically, but literally, 'I found the City of brick, but I leave it of marble.' Constantine the Great was wont to call with envy the Emperor Trajan 'Wall-flower,' because his name was upon so many buildings; which, notwithstanding, he himself did embrace in the new founding of Constantinople, and sundry other buildings: and yet none greater conquerors than these two. And surely they had reason; for the fame of great actions is like to a land-flood, which hath no certain head or spring, but the memory and fame of buildings and foundations hath, as it were, a fountain in an hill, which continually feedeth and refresheth the other waters. Neither do I, excellent Prince, restrain my Speeches to dead buildings only, but intend it also to other foundations, institutions, and creations; wherein I presume the more to speak confidently, because I am warranted herein by your own wisdom, who have made the first fruits of your actions of state, to institute the honourable Order of the Helmet; the less shall I need to say, leaving your Excellency not so much to follow my advice, as your own example."

The Fourth Counsellor, advising Absoluteness of State and Treasure.

"Let it not seem pusillanimity for your Excellency, mighty Prince, to descend a little from your high thoughts to a necessary consideration of your own estate. Neither do you deny, Honourable Lords, to acknowledge safety, profit, and power, to be of the substance of policy, and fame and honour rather to be as flowers of well-ordered actions, than as good guides. Now if you examine the courses propounded according to these respects, it must be confessed, that the course of wars may seem to increase power, and the course of contemplations and foundations not prejudice safety; but if you look beyond the exterior, you shall find that the first breeds weakness, and the latter note peril: for certain it is, during wars, your Excellency will be enforced to your souldiers, and generally to your people, and become less absolute and monarchical than if you reigned in peace; and then if your success be good, that you make new conquests, you shall be constrained to spend the strength of your ancient and settled provinces, to assure you new and doubtful, and become like a strong man, that, by taking a great burden upon his shoulders, maketh himself weaker than he was before. Again, if you think you may not end contemplations with security, your Excellency will be deceived; for such studies will make you retired and disused with your business; whence will follow admiration of your authority; as for the other point, of exercising in every part of your state something new, derived from yourself, it will acquaint your Excellency with an humor of innovation and alteration; which will make your Reign very turbulent and unsettled, and many times your change will be for worse; as in the example last touched, of Constantine, who, by his new translation of his estate, ruinated the Roman Empire. As for profit, there appeareth a direct contrariety betwixt that and all the three courses; for nothing causeth such dissipation of treasure as wars, curiosities, and buildings; and for all this to be recompensed in a supposed honour, a matter apt to be much extolled in words, but not greatly to be praised in conceit, I do think it a loser's bargain. Besides that, many politic

Princes have received as much commendation for their wise and well ordered government, as others have done for their conquests and glorious affections. And more worthy, because the praise of wisdome and judgment is less communicated with fortune. Therefore, excellent Prince, be not transported with shews; follow the order of nature, first to make the most of that you possess, before you seek to purchase more. To put the case by a private man (for I cannot speak high), if a man were born to an hundred pounds by the year, and one shew him how with charge to purchase an hundred pounds more, and another should shew him how without charge to raise that hundred pounds unto five hundred pounds, I should think the latter advice should be followed. The proverb is a countrey proverb, but significative, 'Milk the cow that standeth still; why follow you her that flieth away?' Do not think, excellent Prince, that all the conquests you are to make be foreign; you are to conquer here at home the overgrowing of your grandees in factions, and too great liberties of your people, the great reverence and formalities given to your laws and customs, in derogation of your absolute prerogatives; these and such like be conquests of state, though not of war. You want a Joseph, that should by advice make you the only proprietor of all the lands and wealth of your subjects. The means how to strain up your sovereignty, and how to accumulate treasure and revenue, they are the secrets of your State: I will not enter into them at this place; I wish your Excellency as ready to them, as I know the means ready to perform them."

The Fifth Counsellor, advising him Vertue, and a Graceious Government

"Most Excellent Prince,

"I have heard sundry plats and propositions offered unto you severally: one, to make you a great Prince; another, to make you a strong Prince; and another to make you a memorable Prince; and a fourth, to make you an absolute Prince; but I hear of no mention to make you a good and virtuous Prince; which surely my Lords have left out in discretion, as to arise of your own motion and choice; and so I should have thought, had they not handled their own propositions so artificially and perswadingly, as doth assure me their Speech was not formal. But, most worthy Prince, fame is too light, and profit and surety are too low, and power is either such as you have, or ought not so to seek to have; it is the meriting of your subjects, the making of golden times, the becoming of a natural parent to your State: these are the only and worthy ends of your Grace's virtuous Reign. My Lords have taught you to refer all things to yourself, your greatness, memory, and advantage; but whereunto shall yourself be referred? If you will be heavenly, you must have influence; will you be as a standing pool, that spendeth and choaketh his spring within itself, and hath no streams nor current to bless and make fruitful whole tracts of countreys, whereby it reneweth? Wherefore, first of all, most virtuous Prince, assure yourself of an inward Peace, that the storms without do not disturb any of your repairers of State within; therein use and practise all honourable diversions; that done, visit all the parts of your State, and let the balm distil every where from your Sovereign hands, to the medicining of any part that complaineth, beginning with your seat of State, take order that the fault of your greatness do not rebound upon yourself; have care that your intelligence, which is the light of your State, do not go out, or burn dim or obscure; advance men of virtue, and not of mercenary minds; repress all faction, be it either malign or violent. Then look into the state of your laws, and justice of your land; purge out multiplicity of laws, clear the incertainty of them, repeal those that are snaring, and prize the execution of those that are wholesome and necessary; define the jurisdiction of your Courts, reprize all suits and vexations, all causeless delays and fraudulent shifts and devices, and reform all such abuses of right and justice, assist the ministers thereof, punish severely all extortions and exactions of officers, all corruptions in trials and sentences of judgment. Yet, when you have done all this, think not that the bridle and spur will make the horse to go alone without time and custom. Trust not to your laws for correcting the times, but give all strength to good education; see to the government of your Universities, and all seminaries of youth, and of the private order of families, maintaining due obedience of children towards their parents, and reverence of the younger sort towards the ancient. Then when you have confirmed the noble and vital parts of your realm of State, proceed to take care of the blood and flesh, and good habit of the body. Remedy all decays of population, make provision for the poor, remove all stops in traffick, and all cancers and causes of consumption in trades and mysteries; redress all: but whither do I run, exceeding the bounds of that perhaps I am now demanded? But pardon me, most excellent Prince, for as if I should commend unto your Excellency the beauty of some excellent Lady, I could not so well express it with relation, as if I shewed you her picture; so I esteem the best way to commend a virtuous government, to describe and make appear what it is; but my pencil perhaps disgraceth it: therefore I leave it to your Excellency, to take the picture out of your wise observation, and then to double it, and express it in your government."

The Sixth Councellor, regarding Pass-times and Sports.

"When I heard, most excellent Prince, the three first of my Lords so careful to continue your fame and memory, methought it was as if a man should come to some young Prince, as yourself is; and immediately after his coronation, be in hand with him to make himself a sumptuous and stately tomb. And, to speak out of my soul, I muse how any of your servants can once endure to think of you as of a Prince past. And for my other Lords, who would engage you so deeply in matters of State; the one perswading you to a more absolute, the other to a more gracious Government; I assure your Excellency, their lessons were so cumbersome, as if they would make you a King in a Play; who when one would think he standeth in great majesty and felicity, he is troubled to say his part. What? nothing but tasks? nothing but working-days? No feasting, no music, no dancing, no triumphs, no comedies, no love, no ladies? Let other men's lives be as pilgrimages, because they are tied to divers necessities and duties; but Princes' lives are as Progresses, dedicated only to variety and solace.[1] And if your Excellency should take your barge in a summer evening, or your horse or chariot, to take the air; and if you should do any the honour to visit him; yet your pleasure is the principal, and that is but as it falleth out. So if any of these matters which have been spoken of, fall out in the way of your pleasure, it may be taken; but no otherwise. And therefore, leave your wars to your Lieutenants, and your works and build-

[1] This thought is repeated in Bacon's essay "Of Maſques and Triumphs."

ings to your Surveyors, and your books to your Universities, and your State-matters to your Counsellors, and attend you that in person which you cannot execute by deputy: use the advantage of your youth, be not sullen to your fortune; make your pleasure the distinction of your honours, the studies of your favourites, the talk of your people, and the allurement of all foreign gallants to your Court. And, in a word, sweet Sovereign, dismiss your five Counsellors, and only take Council of your five senses."

"But if a man should follow your five senses (said the Prince) I perceive he might follow your Lordship, now and then, into an inconvenience. Your Lordship is a man of a very lively and pleasant advice; which though one should not be forward to follow, yet it fitteth the time, and what our own humour inclined oftentimes to, delight and merriment. For a Prince should be of a chearful and pleasant spirit; not austere, hard-fronted, and stoical; but, after serious affairs, admitting recreation, and using pleasures, as sauces for meats of better nourishment."

The Prince's Answer and Conclusion to the Speeches of the Counsellors.

"My Lords.

"We thank you for your good opinions; which have been so well set forth, as we should think ourselves not capable of good council, if, in so great variety or perswading reasons, we should suddenly resolve. Mean while, it shall not be amiss to make choice of the last, and upon more deliberation to determine of the rest; and what time we spent in long consulting, in the end we will gain by prompt and speedy executing."

Bibliography

BIBLIOGRAPHY

ABRAM AND SONS. Publishers of the Middle Temple, Its History and Associations (London, 1879).

ADAMS, JOSEPH QUINCY. The Dramatic Records of Sir Henry Herbert, Master of the Revels, 1623–1673 (New Haven, 1917).

ADDISON, C. G. The Knights Templars (2d ed.; London, 1842).

BACON, FRANCIS. Essay XXXVII, Of Maſques and Triumphs.

BAKER, DAVID ERSKINE. Biographia Dramatica (London, 1782).

BARTON, SIR DUNBAR P., bart., and others. The Story of Our Inns of Court (London, 1924).

BELLOT, HUGH H. L. Gray's Inn and Lincoln's Inn (London, 1925).

—— The Inner and Middle Temple (London, 1902).

BIRCH, THOMAS. The Court and Times of James the First (London, 1849).

BLIND, KARL. The Boar's Head at Oxford, and a Teutonic Sun-God, Vol. II, Saga-Book of the Viking Club (London, 1894).

BOAS, FREDERICK S. University Drama in the Tudor Age (Oxford, 1914).

BROWN, BASIL. Law Sports at Gray's Inn (New York, 1921).

CAMPBELL, JOHN, LORD. The Life of Lord Bacon (London, 1853).

—— The Lives of the Chief Justices of England (London, 1849).

—— The Lives of the Lord Chancellors and Keepers of the Great Seal of England (London, 1848).

CHALMERS, GEORGE. An Apology for the Believers in the Shakespeare Papers (London, 1797).

CHAMBERS, E. K. Court Performances before Queen Elizabeth, Modern Language Review II, 1 *et seq.*

—— Notes on the History of the Revels Office under the Tudors (London, 1906).

—— The Elizabethan Stage (Oxford, 1923).

—— The Mediaeval Stage (Oxford, 1903).

COHEN, HERMANN J. A History of the English Bar and Attornatus to 1450 (London, 1929).

COLLIER, J. PAYNE. A Select Collection of Old Plays (London, 1825).

—— The Diary of Philip Henslowe (London, 1845).

—— The History of English Dramatic Poetry to the Time of Shakespeare: and Annals of the Stage (London, 1821).

COURTHOPE, W. J. A History of English Poetry (London, 1897).

CREIZENACH, WILHELM M. A. The English Drama in the Age of Shakespeare (London, 1916).

CUNLIFFE, JOHN W. The Influence of Seneca on Elizabethan Tragedy (London, 1893).

CUNNINGHAM, PETER. Extracts from the Accounts of the Revels at Court, in the Reigns of Queen Elizabeth and King James I (London, 1842).

—— Life of Inigo Jones; edited by James Orchard Halliwell for the Shakespeare Society (London, 1848).
CUNNINGHAM, TIMOTHY. The History and Antiquities of the Four Inns of Court (London, 1780).
DAWSON, W. F. Christmas: Its Origin and Associations (London, 1902).
D'EWES, SIR SIMONDS. The Autobiography and Correspondence of; edited by James Orchard Halliwell (London, 1845).
DILLON, HONORABLE JOHN F. The Inns of Court and Westminster Hall (Des Moines, 1878).
DOUTHWAITE, WILLIAM RALPH. Gray's Inn, Its History and Associations (London, 1886).
DOWNING, WILLIAM. Observations on the Constitution, Customs and Usage of the Honourable Society of the Middle Temple (London, 1896).
DUGDALE, WILLIAM. Origines Juridiciales, or Hiſtorical Memorials of the Engliſh Laws, Courts of Juſtice, etc. (The Savoy, 1671).
EVANS, HERBERT ARTHUR. English Masques (London, 1897).
EVELYN, JOHN. The Diary of (Globe ed.) (London, 1908).
FEUILLERAT, ALBERT. Documents Relating to the Revels at Court, etc. (Louvain, 1914).
FLEAY, FREDERICK GARD. A Biographical Chronicle of the English Drama, 1559–1642 (London, 1891).
—— A Chronicle History of the London Stage (London, 1890).
FLETCHER, REGINALD J. Francis Bacon. Commemoration of his Tercentenary at Gray's Inn (London).
—— The Pension Book of Gray's Inn (London, 1901).
—— The Reformation and the Inns of Court (London, 1903).
FORTESCUE, JOHN. *De Laudibus Legum Angliae* (Cambridge, 1825).
GENEST, JOHN. Some Account of the English Stage from the Restoration in 1660 to 1830 (Bath, 1832).
GOLDSMITH, GEORGE. The English Bar; or Guide to the Inns of Court (London, 1849).
GRAHAM, THOMAS H. B. Gentleman's Magazine, cclxx, 568–580.
GREG, WALTER WILSON. A List of English Plays (London, 1900).
—— A List of Masques, Pageants, etc. (London, 1902).
—— Collections Part II (Lansdowne MSS) (Oxford, 1908).
—— Pastoral Poetry and Pastoral Drama (London, 1906).
—— The Christmas Prince, An Account of the St. John's College Revels Held at Oxford in 1607–8 (The Malone Society Reprints) (Oxford, 1922).
HALL, EDWARD. Chronicle (London, 1809).
HAYWARD, ABRAHAM. Origin and Early History of the Benchers of the Inns of Court (London, 1846).
HAZLITT, W. CAREW. A Select Collection of Old English Plays (London, 1874).
—— The English Drama and Stage, 1543–1664 (Printed for the Roxburghe Library, 1869).

HECKETHORN, CHARLES WILLIAM. Lincoln's Inn Fields and the Localities Adjacent: Their Historical and Topographical Associations (London, 1876).

HENTZNER, PAUL. A Journey into England in the Year M.D.XCVIII (edited by Horace Walpole; reprint of the Aungerville Society, No. II, 1st series) (Edinburgh, 1881).

HERBERT, WILLIAM. Antiquities of the Inns of Court and Chancery (London, 1804).

HILL, CONSTANCE. Good Company in Old Westminster and the Temple (London, 1925).

HOME, GORDON, and HEADLAM, CECIL. The Inns of Court (London, 1909).

HONE, WILLIAM. The Year Book (London, 1832).

HOPE, ANDRÉE. Chronicles of an Old Inn, or, A Few Words about Gray's Inn (London, 1887).

HOPWOOD, CHARLES HENRY. A Calendar of the Middle Temple Records (London, 1903).

HUGHES, THOMAS, and others. The Misfortunes of Arthur; edited with an introduction, notes, and glossary by Harvey Carson Grumbine (Berlin, 1900).

INDERWICK, FREDERICK ANDREW. A Calendar of the Inner Temple Records: Vol. I, 1505–1603 (London, 1896); Vol. II, 1603–1660 (1898); Vol. III, 1660–1714 (1901).

—— The King's Peace, a Historical Sketch of the English Law Courts (Social England Series) (London, 1895).

INGPEN, ARTHUR GEORGE. Worsley's Book on the History and Constitution of the Honourable Society of the Middle Temple (London, 1910) (Master Worsley's Book).

—— The Middle Temple Bench Book (London, 1912).

IRELAND, SAMUEL. Picturesque Views, with an Historical Account of the Inns of Court (London, 1800).

JOHNSON, CUTHBERT WILLIAM. The Life of Sir Edward Coke (London, 1837).

KNIGHT, CHARLES. London (London, 1851).

LAMB, CHARLES. The Old Benchers of the Inner Temple, with annotations by Sir F. D. Mackinnon (Oxford, 1927).

LANE, THOMAS. The Student's Guide through Lincoln's Inn (London, 1823).

LAWRENCE, WILLIAM J. Pre-Restoration Stage Studies (Cambridge, Mass., 1927).

LEGH, GERARD. The Accedens of Armory (London, 1576).

LEIGH, P. BRADY. The Law Student's Guide (London, 1827).

LOFTIE, WILLIAM JOHN. The Inns of Court and Chancery (London, 1893).

LUTTRELL, NARCISSUS. A Brief Historical Relation of State Affairs (Oxford, 1857).

LYON, HASTINGS, and BLOCK, HERMAN. Edward Coke (Boston, 1929).

MACHYN, HENRY. Diary; edited by John Gough Nichols (London, 1848).

MACQUEEN, JOHN FRASER. A Lecture on the Early History and Academic Discipline of the Inns of Court and Chancery (London, 1851).

MAIDMENT, JAMES, and LOGAN, W. H. The Dramatic Works of Sir William d'Avenant (Edinburgh, 1872).

MANNING, JAMES ALEXANDER. Memoirs of Sir Benjamin Rudyerd, Knt., etc. (London, 1841).

MANNINGHAM, JOHN. Diary, 1602–1603; edited by John Bruce (Westminster, 1868).

MARSHALL, THOMAS. A Sketch of the Early History of Legal Practitioners and of the Inns of Court and Chancery (Leeds, 1869).

MELMOTH, WILLIAM. The Great Importance of a Religious Life Considered, etc. (London, 1849).

MORLEY, HENRY. English Plays (London, 1880).

MURRAY, JOHN TUCKER. English Dramatic Companies 1558–1642 (Boston, 1910).

NAUNTON, ROBERT. Fragmenta Regalia. Republished as The Court of Queen Elizabeth (London, 1814).

NICHOLS, JOHN. The Progresses and Public Processions of Queen Elizabeth, &c. (London, 1823).

—— The Progresses, Processions, and Magnificent Festivities of King James the First &c. (London, 1828).

NICOLAS, SIR HARRIS. Memoirs of the Life and Times of Sir Christopher Hatton, M. G. (London, 1847).

NORTH, THE HONORABLE ROGER. The Life of the Right Honorable Francis North, Baron of Guilford, Lord Keeper of the Great Seal under King Charles II and King James II, etc. (London, 1819).

PEARCE, ROBERT R. A History of the Inns of Court and Chancery (London, 1848).

PEPYS, SAMUEL. *Diary.*

PITT-LEWIS, G. The History of "The Temple" with Special References to that of the Middle Temple (London, 1898).

POLLARD AND REDGRAVE. A Short-Title Catalogue of Books Printed in England, Scotland, and Ireland, 1475–1640 (London, 1926).

REYHER, PAUL. *Les Masques Anglais* (Paris, 1909).

Round about Our Coal Fire; or, Christmas Entertainments (London, 1740).

SANDYS, WILLIAM. Christmastide (London, undated).

SCHELLING, FELIX E. Elizabethan Drama, 1558–1642 (Boston, 1908).

Secret History of the Court of James the First, including Sir Anthony Weldon's Court and Character of King James (London, 1811).

SHEPHERD, RICHARD HERNE. The Works of George Chapman (London, 1874).

Six Lectures on the Inns of Court and of Chancery (London, 1912). (W. Blake Odgers, 2; E. M. Underdown; A. R. Ingpen; J. Douglas Walker; and H. E. Duke.)

SOMMERS, JOHN, LORD. A Collection of Scarce and Valuable Tracts Selected Particularly from the Sommers Library (London, 1748).

SPEGHT, THOMAS. The Workes of Ovr Ancient and Learned Englifh Poet, Geffrey Chavcer (London, 1602).

SPILSBURY, WILLIAM HOLDEN. Lincoln's Inn (London, 1850).
STEELE, MARY S. Plays and Masques at Court during the Reigns of Elizabeth, James, and Charles (New Haven, 1926).
STOPES, CHARLOTTE CARMICHAEL. Burbage and Shakespeare's Stage (London, 1913).
—— The Seventeenth Century Accounts of the Masters of the Revels (London, 1922).
—— William Hunnis and the Revels of the Chapel Royal (Louvain, 1910).
STOW, JOHN. The Annales of England (London, 1592).
THOMAS, N. W. Animal Superstitions and Totemism, Folk-lore, Vol. II (London, 1900).
THOMPSON, W. The Works of William Browne (London, 1772).
WALKER, JAMES DOUGLAS. The Records of the Honorable Society of Lincoln's Inn (Black Books) (London, 1897).
WALLACE, CHARLES WILLIAM. The Evolution of the English Drama up to Shakespeare (Berlin, 1912).
WARD, JOHN. Diary, extending from 1648 to 1679; arranged by Charles Severn, M.D. (London, 1839).
WARD, SIR ADOLPHUS WILLIAM. A History of English Dramatic Literature (London, 1899).
WARTON, THOMAS. The History of English Poetry (London, 1774).
WELDON, SIR ANTHONY. The Court of King Charles, supplementing The Court of King James (London, 1661).
WELSFORD, ENID. The Court Masque (Cambridge, England, 1927).
WHITELOCK, SIR BULSTRODE. The History of England, or, Memorials of the English Affairs (London, 1713).
WHITELOCKE, R. H. Memoirs, Biographical and Historical of Bulstrode Whitelocke (London, 1860).
WILLIAMSON, JOHN B. The History of the Temple, London, etc. (London, 1924).

INDEX

Abram, 59
Academy at Inns of Court, 33
Accedens of Armory, 66
"Accretion and Avulsion," 1
Actors, attitude toward, 17
Adamantine Rock, 99
Aeneid, 144
Agricultural feast, 9
Alderson, 5
Alleyn, Edward, 121
Allhallows' Day, 10, 43
All Saints' Day, 10, 43
All Saints' feast, 55
Ambassadors, entertainment of, 40
Ambulatory, 37
American judicial system, 2; legal system, 1; Revolution, 39
Amour, Le Prince de, *see* Prince d'Amour
Amphitrite, 100
Animal Superstitions, 66
Annals of England, 22–24, 48
Antimasques, 15
Apollonius, 113
Apple blossom festival in Virginia, 15
Apprenticii nobiliores, 32
Arcadia, 81
Arcadia, 15
Ariosto, 146
Arthur, Prince, 53
Arthurian legend, 18, 153; romance, 151
Articles of Confederation, adoption of, 2
Arundel, Earl of, 94
Ascension day, 10
As You Like It, 147
Atwell, H., 121
Auditors, 28
Autobiography of Sir Simonds d'Ewes, 92
Autumnalia, 28
"Avulsion and accretion," 1

Baboons, antimasque of, 15, 103
Bacchus, 110
Bacon, Anthony, 82; Francis, 2, 7, 27, 28, 80, 82, 98, 106, 107, 110, 112, 115, 151; Lady, 82
Baldwin, King of Jerusalem, 23
Barnaby Rudge, 8
Barnwell, 5
Barristers, 26
Barton, 82
Beaujoyeulx, 101
Beaumont, Francis, 5, 7, 17, 103–106, 143, 154–156
Bedwell, 26, 28
Beecher, William, 137
Beer, embezzlement of, 35
Bellot, Hugh H. L., 10, 12, 28, 32, 36, 39, 55, 58, 90, 132
Benchers, description of, 26
Bentley, Dr. Richard, 11
Bernardia, 84
Betterton, 155
Birch, Thomas, 36, 94, 105, 107, 109, 112, 136–137
Birth of Merlin, 151
Black Book, 10, 42, 54–58, 65, 89, 138
Blackfriars, 25
Blackmore, solicitor of Gray's Inn, 7
Blackstone, William, 2, 26
Blind, Karl, 65
Boccaccio, Giovanni, 149
Bodleian Library, 85; MS clxviii, 11
Boltings, 40
Bonfires, 54

Bon Voloire, 53
Boston English troops at, 39
Boswell, James, 5
Boucicault, Dion, 154
Boyle lectures, 11
Brent, Nathanael, 120
Brick Court, 6
Bridewell, 36
Bridgewater, Earl of, 116
Bridgman, Sir Orlando, 45
Britannia's Pastorals, 112
British Museum, 62
Brothers, The, 154
Brown, Basil, 71, 99
Browne, John, 121
Browne, William, 4, 17, 112–113
Buckhurst, Thomas Lord, 80, 142
Buckingham, Duke of, 45
Buckingham, Earl of, 136
Buckley, Master, 3
Bucks for Reader's Feast, 47
Bulwer-Lytton, Edward, 6
Burgundy, son of the duke, 53
Burleigh, Lord, 80
Butler, Samuel, 6, 57
Byles on Bills, 5
Byron, Lord, 39

Calderón de la Barca, Pedro, 149
Calendar of Inner Temple Records, 153
Calendar of State Papers, 91
Callis on Sewers, 28
Cambridge University, 3, 11, 25, 35
Camden, William, 7
Campbell, John, 7
Campion, Thomas, 99–101, 105, 109
Candlemas Day, 10, 12, 15, 43
Canning, W., 72
Canterbury, Archbishop of, 40, 46
Capriccio, 104
Captivi, 147
Carleton, Mrs. Dudley, 105; Sir Dudley, 36, 105, 107, 109, 112, 117, 120, 137
Carpenter, W., 121
Carr, Robert, 109
Cat, 66
Catherine, Queen, *see* Katherine, Queen
Cecil, Robert, 80; William, 72
Chalmers, George, 20
Chamberlain, John, 36, 105, 107, 112, 117
Chambers, E. K., 62, 66, 85, 149
Chancery Lane, 23, 25
Changes, The, 154
Chapman, George, 7, 103, 105
Charity of Inns of Court, 31
Charles, I, 15, 54, 134, 137; II, 10, 41, 47, 56, 62, 89, 135, 156; Prince Palatine, 132
Chaucer, Geoffrey, 3–4
Cheats of Scapin, The, 156
Chichester, Bishops of, 25
Childermas Day, 12
Chitty, 5
Christmas, 15; prince, 100; regulations concerning, 95; revels, 12
Chronicle of Edward Hall, 16, 97
Clarendon, Lord Chancellor, 126
Clarissa Harlowe, 6
Clark, Richard, 35
Classical drama, 18–19; play and English morality, 20
Cleomenes, 46
Clericus Coquinae, 57
Clerk of the kitchen, 57
Cleveland, John, 7
Clown, The, 154
Cockneys, king of, 12
Coke, Edward, 2, 5, 27; John, 38; Thomas, 125
Collaboration, 21
Collier, John Payne, 117, 151
Collins, William Wilkie, 7
Colonies, American, 2
Comedy of Errors, 8, 80, 154
Comfits, 48
Comical Revenge, The, 154
Committee, The, 155

Compton, Lord, 80, 82
Comus, 116, 134
Conference of Pleasure, The, 98
Congreve, William, 5
Constable of the Tower, 57
Constabularius Turris, 57
Constantine, 22
Constitution of the United States, signatories of, 2
Continental Congress, 2
Corpus Christi Day, 9
Council of Troyes, 31
Countryman, The, 154
Courants, 44
Court, Inns of, *see* Inns of Court
Covent Garden Journal, 65
Coventry, Thomas Lord, 131
Cowper, Earl of, 125
Cowper, William, 5
Creizenach, Wilhelm M. A., 149
Criminals, 36
Cross, Holy, 22
Crow, "Fridaysweed," 38; "Pennifeather," 38
Crusaders, 22
Crypt, 37
Cullum, Sir Thomas Gery, 135
Cumberland, Earl of, 80
Cure Loial, 53

Damon and Pithias, 153
Dance of the Nations, 138
Darrel, Mr., 127
Davenant, William, 17, 102, 117, 133, 134, 154
David Copperfield, 8
Davison, Francis, 99, 101
Dawson, W. F., 56, 58, 62, 66, 90, 94
Daye, John, 142
Decameron, 149
Declaration of Independence, signers of, 2
de Coverley, Sir Roger, 5
Defence of Poesie, 145
De Laudibus Legum Angliae, 27, 33
de Quincey, Thomas, 5
"Devil's Own!" 4
Devonshire, Earl of, 53, 117
D'Ewes, Richard, 37
d'Ewes, Sir Simonds, 92
Diana, 65
Diary, John Evelyn, 89, 92; Narcissus Luttrell, 135; Henry Machyn, 71, 142; Samuel Pepys, 95
Dicing, 15, 90, 92
Dickens, Charles, 7
Dillon, John F., 26
Diogenes, 155
Disraeli, Benjamin, 2
Diversions of members of Inns of Court, 1
Dolce, M. Lodovico, 146
Don Quixote, 130
Dorset, Earl of, 143
"Double Reader," 42
Douthwaite, William Ralph, 109, 120
Drama, characters of classical, 19; courtly, 19; distinctiveness of the product of the Inns of Court, 19; English classical, 19; sensational, 19
Dry, 38
Dryden, John, 7, 149, 154–156
Dudley, Robert, 68
Dugdale, William, 10–12, 30, 37, 42–43, 45, 48–51, 66, 93, 109
Durfey, Tom, 156
Dyce, Alexander, 121

Echo, 19, 115
Edward, Prince, 27; III, 24; IV, 53
Edwards, Richard, 153
'Εγκυκλοχρέια, 138
Eldon, 5
Elector Palatine, 15
Elizabeth, Princess, 7, 15, 39, 93, 102, 105; Queen, 11, 32, 81, 84, 98, 100, 104, 142, 144, 147, 150

Elizabethan stage, 149
Ely House, 51, 127
England and the United States, governmental relationship, 2
English classical drama, 18; legal system, 1; literature and Inns of Court, 1; troops at Boston, 39
Epicene, 154
Epiphany, the, 15
Esquire, 100
Essex, Countess of, 15, 109, 112; Earl of, 80, 109
Etherege, George, 154
Eugenius, Pope, 23
Eunuchus, 147
Euripides, 146, 152
Evans, Herbert Arthur, 110, 116, 128
Evelyn, John, 5, 40, 88–89, 91–92
Every Man Out of His Humor, 6
Expenses at Inns of Court, 33

Fables, 149
Faerie Queene, 8
Faithorne's Tavern, 89
Fawkes, Guy, 54
Feast, reader's, 28, 40; sergeants', 48; All Saints' and the Purification, 55
Ferrex and Porrex, 142
Festival, apple blossom in Virginia, 15
Fielding, Henry, 6; Lady Elizabeth, 134
Finch, Sir Heneage, 45; Sir John, 126, 131
Fleay, Frederick Gard, 7, 98, 117, 134, 136
Fleet Street, 54
Fleire, The, 154
Fletcher, Reginald J., 11, 35, 47, 56, 58, 109, 135, 143, 154, 155, 156
Florimel, 155
Flower, Francis, 151
Flowers, Masque of, 109–110, 112
Folk-lore, 66
Fond Husband, The, 156
Food for sergeants' feast, 51
Forest laws, 28
Fortescue, John, 2, 27, 33, 48
Foundlings, maintenance of, 37
Fourberies de Scapin, Les, 156
Fox, 66
Freyja, 64
Fulbeck, William, 151

Galiatto, 81
Galliards, 44
Gammer Gurton's Needle, 147
Garrard, G., 57
Garrick, David, 156
Gascoigne, George, 7, 145–146, 149
Gayley, Charles Mills, 17
Geoffrey of Monmouth, 144, 151
George III, 4
Gerling, Mr., 126
Gesta Grayorum, 7, 71, 80, 100, 101, 117
Giocasta, 146
Gipps, Sir Richard, 135
Gismonde of Salerne, 149
Gli Sopposití, 146
Goldsmith, George, 49; Oliver, 5–6
Goodricke, Sir Francis, 41
Gorboduc, 17, 21, 142–146, 148–153
Gordon, Duke of, 89
Goring, Lord, 134
Gower, John, 3
Grace Book of Inner Temple, 30
Graham, Thomas H. B., 26
Graius, 81
"Grand Days," 11
Grange, de la, 138
Gray, Lady Anne, 148; Thomas, 145; of Wilton, lords, 25
Gray's Inn, 34, 101; conciliation of Inner Temple, 14; hall, 32; history of, 25; plate, 36; products of, 7; reading, 47, sergeants' feast, 48

Gray's Inn and Inner-Temple Masque, 5, 105, 135
Greek language, study of, 3
Griffith, William, 142
Grillus, 114
Ground-hog day, 10
Grumbine, 151–152
Guild system, 9, 29
Guizot, 81
Gustavus, 5
Gwillim, 59
Gwyn, Eleanor, 61, 155
Gymnasium at Inns of Court, 33

Hall, Edward, 16, 53, 97
Hall, The, 59
Hallam, Arthur Henry, 5
Hamilton, Marchioness, 134
Hargrave MS, 148
Harris, Dr. J., 11
Hatton, Christopher, 69, 145, 147
Hawley, 36
Hazlitt, William, 148, 149
Heckethorn, Charles William, 37
Hecuba, 152
Helena, 22
Henneage, Sir Thomas, 80
Henry, Prince of Wales, 137; I, 23; VI, 10, 31; VIII, 9, 51, 53, 97
Hentzner, Paul, 33
Herbert, Sir Edward 126; Sir Gerrard, 120; Henry, 134; Philip, 131; William, 11–13, 25, 31, 41, 42, 51, 53, 54, 124
Heroes, Masque of, 121
Heroic play, Latin, 13
Hipocras, 43, 136
History of the British Kings, 144, 151
Histriomastix, 15, 124
Holborn, 23, 25
Holiday revels, 12
Holinshed, Raphael, 151
Holland, Earl of, 58, 134
Holmes, Henry, 72
Homer, 113
Honorius, Pope, 23
Hooker, James, 58
Hopwood, Charles Henry, 36, 38, 90, 105
Hospitalers of St. John, 24
Howard, Robert, 155; Lord Thomas, 80
Hudibras, 6
Hughes, Thomas, 5, 151–153
Hyde, Edward, 126
Hyginus, 113
Hylham, John, 35
Hymenaei, 109

Inderwick, Frederick Andrew, 10, 11, 16, 25–32, 35–40, 47, 48, 54–56, 59–60, 65, 90, 91, 93, 95, 96, 109, 116, 123, 125, 138, 147, 153
Inner Temple, affront by Middle Temple, 29; Chaucer as member of, 3; conciliation of, by Gray's Inn, 14; General Account Book, 54; Grace Book, 30; Records, 38; residents of, 4; separation from Middle Temple, 25; training school, 4
Inner-Temple and Gray's Inn Masque, 5, 105
Inner Temple Masque, 4–5, 112, 121
Inns of Chancery, subordinate to Inns of Court, 25
Inns of Court, charity of, 31; curriculum of, 2; description of, 27; diversion of members, 1; drama of, 19; Dugdale's description of, 30; equality of, 25; expenses at, 33; Fortescue's description of, 33; governing bodies of, 27; Hentzner's description of, 34; indebtedness of America to, 2; internal organization of, 22, 25; literature of, 1, 3, 8; "nurseries of humanity," 6; pedanticism of,

19; postgraduate institutions, 35; rise of, 22; sermons, 11
Invierno, 110
Ives, Simon, 126, 127

Jack Straw, 56
James, I, 102, 108, 110; II, 54
Jerusalem, road to, 22
Jocasta, 7, 17, 145–147
Johnson, Samuel, 6, 7
Jones, Inigo, 17, 101, 103
Jonson, Ben, 6, 20, 101, 109, 131, 154
Journey Into England in the Year MDXCVII, 34
Jousts, 53, 54
"Judicial University," 25
Jupiter, 19

Katherine, Queen, 51, 53
Kawasha, 110, 111
Kentish Town, 65, 72
Kidder, Bishop, 11
King of cockneys, 12, 56
King's Head Tavern, 54, 60
Kingsley, Charles, 7
Kinwelmarsh, Francis, 146
Knevet, Sir Thomas, 53
Knight, William, 37
Knights Templars, battle chant, 22; description, 6, 9, 23, 24, 31
Kyd, Thomas, 152

Lacy, Henry, Earl of Lincoln, 25
Lamb, Charles, 5
Lambard, Sir Nicholas, 51
Lancaster, Earl of, 24; John, 151
Landsdowne MS, 148
"Last clear chance," 1
Latin, heroic play, 13; study of, 3
Law and philosophy, 29; United States, 2
Lawes, Henry, 126, 134; William, 126, 127, 134
Lawrence, William J., 19, 117, 146
Law Sports at Gray's Inn, 71
Laws, forest, 28
Leake, William, 86
Lear, King, 144
Lector, 28
Legal guild system, 29; procedure, satire of, 1; English and American, 1
Legh, Gerard, 66, 98
Leicester, Earl of, 68
Lent, 40; reader for, 41
L'Étourdi, 155
Lieutenant of the Tower, 11
Lincoln, Abraham, 2; Earl of, 25
Lincoln's Inn, 34; history of, 25; products of, 6; revels of, 10; Samuel Butler's description of, 6; under-barristers of, 12
Lincoln's Inn and Middle Temple Masque, 102
Literary centers in Inns of Court, 3
Literature, dramatic, 2; Inns of Court, 1
Little French Lawyer, The, 155
Little Thief, The, 154
Littleton, Lord Keeper, 137; Thomas, 2
Liveries, 50
London Cuckolds, The, 155
Lope Felix de Vega Carpio, 149
Lord of misrule, 11
Lord's Masque, The, 105
Lort, Mr., 89
Love in a Maze, 154
Love in a Tub, 154
Love Lyes a Bleeding, 155
Lowe, George, 116
Lower, Mr., 93
Loyal Protestant, 135
Lucan, 132
Luttrell, Narcissus, 33, 89, 135
Lyon's Inn, 29

Macaulay, Thomas Babington, 6
Machyn, Henry, 71, 142
Magister Jocorum, 11
Magistri de Banco, 26

Maiden Queen, The, 155
Manciple's Tale, 4
Manfred, 39
Manning, J. A., 102
Manwood, Roger, 68
Marescallus, 57
Marriage of the Thames and the Rhine, 105
Marshal, 57
Marshall, John, 2
Marston, John, 117
Martino, Sir, 88
Mary, Queen, 156
Masque, 13; definition of, 15, 16; use as tribute, 16
Masque, Inner Temple, The, 4–5
Masque, Lords', The, 105
Masque of 1526, The, 97
Masque of 1565–66, The, 98
Masque of 1592, The, 98
Masque of Amity, The, 14
Masque of Flowers, The, 7, 15, 109, 110, 112
Masque of Heroes, The, 121, 123
Masque of Mountebanks, The, 117, 120
Masque of Proteus, The, 72, 85, 98, 99, 104, 113, 114
Masque of the Inner-Temple and Gray's Inn, 105, 109
Masque of the Inner-Temple, The, 112, 121
Masque of the Middle Temple and Lincoln's Inn, The, 102, 103, 126
Masque of the Nine Passions, 102
Masque, The, 97
Masques and Triumphs, 115
Massachusetts, 2
Master and servant, 1
Master of the revels, 11
Mathematics, study of, 3
Maxwell, 36
May, Thomas, 132
May Day, 15
Mead, Joseph, 94, 136
Melmoth, 11, 39
Menaechmi, 79
Merry Boys of Christmas, 61
Metamorphoses, 19
Middle Temple, 25; affront to Inner Temple, 29; hall, 6; Records, 47, 90; residents, 5
Middle Temple and Lincoln's Inn Masque, 102
Middleton, Thomas, 17, 121
Midsummer day, 10
Milton, John, 116, 134
Miracle play, 9
Misanthrope, Le, 156
Misfortunes of Arthur, 18, 21, 144, 146, 150, 151, 152, 153
Misrule, lord of, 11
Molière, 155, 156
Moot, 28, 40
Morality play and classical play, 20
More, Sir Thomas, 6
Morte D'Arthur, 151
Mounteagle, Lord, 80
Mountebanks, Masque of, 117
Mountjoy, Lord, 80
Moyle, Thomas, 98
Mulcting, 13
Mumming, 15, 65
Musicians, 11
Mystery play, 9

Nations, Dance of, 38
Naunton, Robert, 145
Neville, Sir Edward, 53
New England, 40
New Inn, 44
Newton, J., 121
New Year's revels, 12
Nichols, John, 40, 66, 71, 73, 74, 80, 84, 93, 103, 105, 107, 135–137
Nicolas, 112, 117
Night of Errors, 80
Night Walker, The, 154
Nine Passions, The Masque of, 102
Noctes Templariae, 85

North, Francis, 3, 45, 46; Roger, 3, 45
Northumberland, Earl of, 80
Norton, George, 103; Thomas, 4, 143, 144, 151
Novelists, nineteenth-century, 5
Noy, Attorney-General, 126, 127
Nuntius, 152

Odyssey, 113
Of Masques and Triumphs, 7
Oldbourne, 23
Old English Plays, 148
Olympus, 15
Orange, Prince of, 89
Organization of Inns of Court, 22
Origines Juridiciales, 30, 43
Ormond, Duke of, 45
Otway, Thomas, 156
Ovid (Publius Ovidius Naso), 19, 113
Owls, antimasque of, 15
Oxford Tragedy, 154
Oxford University, 3, 11, 20, 25, 35, 39

Pagan agricultural feast, 9
Paganus, 23
Pageant, legal, 10; religious, 10
Palaphilos, 69
Palatine, Count, 102
Palmer, Mr., 94
Paris, Matthew, 24
Passions, The Nine, 102
Pegasus, Order of, 69
Pembroke, Earl of, 132
Pendennis, 5
Penruddock, 151
Pensioners, 28
Pepys, Samuel, 92, 95, 154, 155
Peter, Lady Mary, 148; the Great, 89
Pewter, 36
Philaster, 155
Philips, Sir Edward, 103, 109
Philosophy and the law, 29
Phoenissae, The, 146
Pickwick Papers, 8
Pilgrimages to Jerusalem, 22
Pincerna, 57
Pitt-Lewis, G., 29, 47, 136
Plain Dealer, The, 156
Plate at Gray's Inn, 36
Plautus, 79, 147
Play, amount paid for, 20
Players, pay of, 90
Plotting Sisters, The, 156
Plutarch, 81
Political Revels, 53
Polydorus, 152
Pope, Alexander, 145
Portugal, 54
Posthumous Papers of the Pickwick Club, 8
Post Revels, 12, 44
Potations, 31
Presents given by sergeants, 50
Primavera, 110
Prince, Christmas, 100; d'Amour, 56, 85; de la Grange, 56; of Orange, 10; of Purpoole, 56; of Sophie, 56
Prince d'Amour, 86, 102, 126, 132, 134
Professional Revels, 40
Proserpina, 19
Proteus, 100
Proteus, Masque of, 72, 98, 99
Prothalamion, 6
Prynne, William, 15, 123, 124, 125
Psalm, quoting of, 43
Purification, day, 39, 43; feast of, 10, 55
Purpoole, Prince of, 56, 73, 74

Quadragesima, 28

Ralph Roister Doister, 147
Rasselas, 7
Ravenscroft, Edward, 155
Reader, double, 42; feast of, 28,

40; Lent, 41; office of, 28; summer, 44
Return from Parnassus, 19
Revels, definition of, 13; master of, 11; political, 53; post, 44; professional, 40
Revolution, American, 39
Rich, Lord, 80; Mr., 89
Richard II, 3
Richardson, Samuel, 6
Richmond, Duke of, 45, 89
Rings, gold, 50
Rise of Inns of Court, 22
Ritual, legal, 14
Robinson, Richard, 39; Robert, 150
Rochester, Bishop of, 11; Lord, 54, 112
Roister Doister, see Ralph Roister Doister
Roo, John, 97
Round About Our Coal Fire, 63
Rowley, William, 121, 151
Rudyerd, Benjamin, 85, 102
Rule a Wife and Have a Wife, 156
Rupert, Prince, 132
Rymer, Thomas, 7

Sackville, Thomas, 4, 143, 144, 151
Saga-Book of the Viking Club, 65
St. Erkenwald, 10
St. John, hospitalers of, 24
St. Omer, Godfrey de, 22
St. Paul's School, 84
St. Thomas' Eve, 12
Salisbury, Earl of, 58
Salmacida Spolia, 117
Sanctuary, right of, 38
Sandys, William, 64
Saracen, 22
Satire of legal procedure, 1
Saturnalia of 1526, 97
Saunders, William, 32
Scales, Lord, 53
Schelling, Felix E., 147
Scornful Lady, The, 155
Secret Love, 155
Segismonda and Guiscardo, 149
Selden, John, 126
Seneca, 152, 153
Sepulcher, Holy, 22
Sergeant-at-Law's Tale, 4
Sergeants, elect, 49; feast, 48
Sergeants' Inn, 48, 49
Sermons at Inns of Court, 11
Servant and master, 1
Servius, 113
Sewers, 28
Shakespeare, Society, 117; William, 20, 80, 147, 149, 151, 152, 154, 156; *Comedy of Errors*, 8; *Twelfth Night*, 6
Sharpham, Mr., 154
Sheffield, Lord, 80
Sheldon, Archbishop, 46
Shene, prior and convent of, 25
Shepherd, Richard Herne, 103
Shirley, James, 14, 25, 103, 123, 129, 134, 154
Shooting at Inns of Court, 35
Shrewsbury, Earl of, 80
Shrove Tuesday, 15
Sidney, Sir Philip, 7, 145
Silent Woman, The, 154
Silenus, 110
Silver, 36
Sir Martin Mar-All, 155
Smith's Leading Cases, 5
Society of the Inner Temple, *see* Inner Temple
Soldier's Fortune, The, 156
"Soldiers of Justice," 24, 30
"Solemn revels," 12
Solomon as aide to Gustavus, 5
Somerset, Earl of, 15, 89, 109
Southampton, Earl of, 80
Spanish Curate, The, 155
Spanish Friar, The, 156
Spanish Priest, The, 156
Spectator, Mr., 5
Spedding, James, 80, 82, 98
Speght, Thomas, 3
Spencer, Sir John, 82

Spenser, Edmund, 6
"Spread," 40
Staple Inn, 7
Stapleton, Richard, 26
Stapulia, 84
State Papers, 109, 120, 137
Statute of Uses, 28
Steele, Mary S., 86, 102, 117, 136
Stephen, King, 29
Stevenson, William, 147
Steward, 12
Stopes, Charlotte Carmichael, 11
Stow, John, 22, 24, 48
Stradilax, Milorsius, 88, 102
Strafford, Earl of, 57
Strangers at Inns of Court, 35
Stuarts, 16
Students, 26
Studies, 32
Stuteville, Sir Martin, 94, 136
Summer readers, 44
Supposes, The, 7, 17, 146, 147, 149
System, American judical, 2

Tale of the Manciple, 4
Tale of the Sergeant-at-Law, 4
Taming of the Shrew, The, 147, 156
Tancred and Gismund, 17, 21, 147, 148, 149, 150, 152, 153
Tantalus, 152
Taylor, Joseph, 121
Templarius, 81
Temple, at Jerusalem, 22, 34; Christmas, 38; family name, 38; Garden, 5; Gate, 54; New, 23; Old, 23
Terence, 147
Thackeray, William Makepeace, 5
Thames, Marriage of, 105
Thamesis, 100
Thesaurarius, 27
Thomas, Earl of Lancaster, 24; N. W., 66
Thorpe, Mr., 36
Thyestes, 152
Tiltings and joustings, 54
Tityus, 92
Tower, lieutenant of, 11
Travesty of legal customs, 13
Treasurer, 27
Treherne on forest laws, 28
Trinity, 11; College, Cambridge, 11
Tripbook, Robert, 56
Triumph of Peace, The, 14, 15, 25, 103, 123, 126, 128, 131, 132, 134
Triumphs of the Prince d'Amour, see *Prince d'Amour*
Troops, English, at Boston, 39
Trotte, Nicholas, 151
Troyes, Council of, 31
Tudors, 16
Tuke, Brian, 26
Twelfth Night, 80, 154, 156
Tyler, Anne, 58
Tyndall, Sir John, 36

Udall, Nicholas, 147
Ulysses and Circe, 104, 111–113, 116
United States, Constitution of, 2; governmental relationship with England, 2; law of, 2
Urban, Pope, 22
Uses, Statute of, 28

Valence, Aimer de, 24
Valiaunt Desire, 53
Victoria, Queen, 112
Viking-Club, Saga-Book of the, 65
Virgil, 113
Virginia, 2; apple blossom festival, 15

Ward, Adolphus William, 114, 146, 151
Webbe, William, 148
Welsford, Enid, 13, 15, 16, 57, 62, 66, 117
Westminster, 49, 54

Whitehall, 45
Whitelock, Bulstrode, 88, 124, 126, 127, 128, 131
Whitelocke, R. H., 88, 124, 126, 127
Widener Library, 85
Wideville, Lord Scales, 53
William and Mary, 54
Williams, Bishop, 11
Williamson, John B., 22, 26–28, 31, 32, 47, 53, 57, 89, 91, 93, 94, 137, 147, 148
Windsor, Lord, 80
Wit Without Money, 154
Wolsey, Cardinal Thomas, 97
Women, exclusion of, 32
Wood, Richard, 31
Worcester, Marquis of, 89
Wycherley, William, 5, 156

Yelverton, Christopher, 151; Henry, 112
York, Duke of, 45, 125
Yorkshire Tragedy, 154